MW01147592

Alive Again...
Again...and Again

This book is dedicated to my husband, Robert, who has supported me emotionally and financially throughout this project.

Alive Again...
Again...and Again

43 Actual Past Life Regressions and How They Can Help You

Pat Rowe Corrington

Awakening Publications
Danville, California

Copyright ©1995, Pat Corrington. All rights reserved.
First Edition published 1995

No part of this work may be reproduced in any form, or by any means, without the permission of the publisher. Exceptions are made for brief excerpts to be used in published reviews.

Published by **Awakening Publications**
696 San Ramon Valley Blvd. #402
Danville, CA 94526

ISBN: 0-9647606-8-1
Library of Congress Catalog Card Number: 95-78460

Printed in the United States of America
by Griffin Printing, Penny Hancock
Sacramento, CA

This book is available at retail stores, by phone
or from order forms in the back of the book.
Credit Cards are welcome.
For credit card orders call: (800) 352-6657.
For international orders call: (602) 650-8442
For information call: (602) 241-6677.

The names of clients in this book are not the names of the actual persons. These names are fictitious. Every attempt has been made to protect the privacy of clients. This publication is for information only and is not intended to provide treatment. If treatment is needed, please consult the appropriate professional.

COVER DESIGN: Lightbourne Images
INTERIOR DESIGN: Lightbourne Images
LOGO DESIGN: From a painting, *The Awakening*, by Ann Marie Eastburn of *Mystic Impressions* and adapted for logo by Carol Ann Flores.

10 9 8 7 6 5 4 3 2 1

Acknowledgments

*F*or those who contributed their time and effort in the production of this book I give you a heartfelt thank you: to my friend, Carol Ann Flores, for guiding me in the purchasing of equipment and in the layout of the book; to my step-mother, Cecilia Rowe, for giving me the inspiration to go ahead; to Penny Webster Scholton and Geoff Fullick for editing; and to Patty O'loan and her friend, Toni Ellis, who offered encouragement. To Patricia Evans, author of *The Verbally Abusive Relationship, How to Recognize it and How to Respond*, (Bob Adams, Inc., 1992), and *Verbal Abuse Survivors Speak Out*, (Bob Adams, Inc., 1993), I thank you for your expertise and advice. Len and Yvonne Fisher offered encouragement and found a quote I could not locate. Stephen Sanders helped me find a quote from William Shakespeare and his mother, Margaret Sanders, helped me by being my resident Doubting Thomas.

Thank you to the Pebble Beach Company for giving me permission to use the name of their resort in one of the chapters.

To my family, husband Robert, and daughters, Debbie Corrington and Kim Guptill, I thank you for understanding about the need to immerse myself in this work. To grand-daughters, Amber and Alexxa, I offer you the challenge to make your dreams come true no matter how long it takes.

A special thank you to Thomas Edison whose inspiration pushed me to *just do it*.

Foreword

*M*ost organized religions of the world embrace a belief in an after life. That we continue to exist, if not taken for granted, is at least accepted as a viable possibility. Why then is it so difficult to believe that there is also a pre–life?

In *Alive Again...Again...and Again*, Pat Rowe Corrington has opened the door to this alternate possibility of reality. She believes it is conceivable that we live through many lifetimes and that memories of these lifetimes are retained at some level. It has been her experience in her many therapy sessions that a client can be regressed back to those previous lifetimes in order to deal with emotional, physical and spiritual problems occurring in his/her current life.

In *From Erin With Love: Knowledge of Life After Death*, I have written about my daughter's illness, her subsequent death, and the fulfillment of a promise made that she would let us know if there was indeed a continuation of life. In my book I have included automatic writings from Erin that validate Pat Rowe Corrington's hypothesis.

Among Erin's messages are interspersed phrases such as: "No more my time; many lives before to then; many lives to do; many lives we have." Through this same type of writing, our family has received this powerful confirmation. "We are all one in the eyes of God. Realizing there are many lifetimes to learn lessons is lesson unto itself."

The concept of past lives tends to give more of a purpose to our lives, that we are here for a reason rather than: we come from nothing; we are born; we struggle through the roller coaster peaks and valleys of life; we die; we return to nothing. Consider perhaps instead that we are here to grow in understanding and to work toward eliminating the factors that restrain us from realizing our full potential as spiritual beings.

One of the theories of reincarnation is that we replay each life with many of the same people each time around. Gender and race often change, but the part of us that I call the soul, or the essence of a person, remains the same (my experiences since Erin's earth death support this as she has obviously retained her memory, her personality and her love for her family). Only the body, the vehicle for the soul, changes. This could explain the sense of knowing someone the first time you meet or the feeling of deja vu when you are in a locale you have never before frequented. This certainly gives you a different twist to the current fad phrase, "Been there, done that." Pat Rowe Corrington's book points dramatically in that direction.

We may have to replay our lives again and again to learn a concept as simple as how to really care for each other. My inclination is to believe that this is the ultimate reason we are in what might be defined as earth school. What a beautiful world it would be if we all took the time to really see our fellow man and not be so quick to judge. Who knows, in the next life you may come back as an individual similar to the one you are now judging so negatively. Perhaps the statement, "Don't judge a man a until you have walked in his shoes" should be changed to "Don't judge a man until you have walked in his earth suit."

Pat Rowe Corrington is about to take you on a journey but she will let you choose the path. One path will lead you to believe, as I do, that life is continuation, that we have lived many times and that memories of those past lives survive within our sub–conscious or soul, whichever you prefer.

You may choose to believe that the many people who have been regressed over the years have been able to tap into an as yet unidentified part of the mind. You may subscribe to the theory that when the right channels have been unblocked each of us has the power to not only identify and name our emotional hang–ups, but also to write an acceptable and inventive scenario that dramatizes the cause.

Regardless of the path you choose to follow in coming to terms with what you are about to read, it is important to understand that the essential benefit to those who have been regressed is, in my estimation, relief that the reason they have acted or thought a certain way has been due to a specific, perhaps traumatic, event in their pre–life. Once you have an understandable explanation you are empowered to make positive changes, the roadblock has been lifted. To me, this is a healthy and powerful form of psychotherapy. It allows you to understand and not blame. How can you blame someone for sins committed against you in another life?

Once you have completed this journey with Pat Rowe Corrington you may find yourself more open to other explanations of things physical and metaphysical; things psychological and mythological. You may find that your real journey towards personal growth and spiritual enlightenment has just begun.

Helen M. Fisher
1995

Table of Contents

Introduction

It is as though I have been cast in a role and the
play has already begun and I can't leave the stage.

What do you believe about the world and your
place in it? **What you believe on faith is as
personal to you as is your fingerprint.** You
cannot be forced to believe that which is not consistent with
your life experiences. Faith in certain belief systems seems to
develop partly from your environment and from intrinsic
knowledge. **Intrinsic knowledge refers to that knowledge
that seems to be a part of you like your eye color and is just
known. Many people may have an intrinsic knowledge of
some things such as God or an afterlife—others may not.**
No person or group of people have the right to force another
person or group of people to believe that which is not consistent with their life experiences or their own intrinsic
knowledge. In the same way, no person or group of people
have the right to force others who have come to certain belief

systems to deny them because some have not come to those same conclusions unless, of course, beliefs have developed which bring harm to the self or to others.

Some of you may find your life experiences do not seem to support your beliefs, and, rather than be fooled or deceived, you prefer to give no credence to those beliefs unless science proves otherwise. Others find life experiences continually supporting belief systems and urging deeper exploration. A belief in an emerging **Western View of Reincarnation** is one of those beliefs that seems to come to be accepted by many as they explore their own spirituality. As you learn more and more about yourself and others, the philosophy may begin to make sense to you as well.

This book is about healing the self and taking control of your life. That is done through self-knowledge. **The more you understand the self, the more you understand others. Many past-life regressions are presented in this book to give you insight into the various kinds of experiences humans can have on the earth plane.**

When I work with clients using past-life regression, I take notes by hand so that I have a transcript to hand the person when they leave. Therefore, the regressions you see in this book are from my notes and are not taken from audiotapes. Years ago I found that transcribing audiotapes was a terrible waste of time. Clients are much more likely to read their notes from a session than they are to sit down and replay an hour tape. Since I am conducting the session as I am taking notes, I miss words and, upon occasion, whole sentences. Sometimes I add material from memory which I had not written. So, one would say the regressions in this book are fairly accurate transcripts of actual sessions.

Names, dates and places have been changed so that clients cannot be identified.

An example of a regression which has to do with faith is about to follow. This is to give you a taste of what to expect later in the book. Our client is one who has developed substantially over time, exploring her spirituality and improving her intuitive skills. Through many of her lifetimes, which we had previously viewed through earlier past-life regressions, she has consistently been a person of the utmost integrity. Though she had been quite accurate with intuitive information and impressions she had received, she had moments of doubting the validity of her information. This is a phenomenon quite common to teachers, writers, students and channels who are guided or inspired. Such was the nature of the perceived problem for our client on this particular visit.

Regression procedures will be explained later in the book. **Prayer, relaxation, guided meditation and chakra balancing are part of this whole process because, as is emphasized in the book, this is a spiritual process and should be treated as such.** Regressions will be indented and italicized throughout the book. My questions and clarifying comments will be italicized in parenthesis within the text of the regression. As noted earlier, all identifying information has been changed.

STORIES AS PARABLES

Use the stories as parables—stories that teach about the human experience in all its richness and diversity, pain and joy. A fascinating story about faith follows. Remember, our client was experiencing doubts about her own faith. It was important to her that any information she shared with another person be absolutely accurate and delivered with the purist of motives. She was instructed to go back to another time when she had had those same feelings.

(You are moving along a path as though you are moving in slow motion. You are moving along a path at a more normal pace now and you notice the vegetation on either side of the path. What do you see?) Actually, I see a stone fence to my right, made of field stones, about 2 feet high. The road is not paved. It is packed dirt, but it is a road, not a foot path. I am walking towards town. There is much activity along the road. There are horses and carts. People are taking things to the city to sell and leaving with things they have purchased.

I believe I'm a monk. I have a walking staff. I am looking down. I have no sandals. I see my robe with a beaded sash and a rope to secure it. Around my neck I wear a crucifix.

(Are you going to walk into town?) Yes. I seem to be greeted by individuals as I pass.

(Do they know you?) Yes. There is much activity along this road. It must be market day. There is much coming and going.

(Are you going to market?) Yes. I sense that I'm going in to preach.

(Where do you preach?) I see myself right in the market, outside. I see stone walls and hay. The carts appear to be very simplistic. Wooden wheels. I see very little metal on them. Most of the people around me appear to be working class, perhaps working class poor farmers, laborers. So, I go to where I know they'll be.

(What is your message for them?) Hope. They work very hard and gain little. They view themselves as powerless. So, I bring them a message of hope—that their pain in this life will gain them entrance in the afterlife with God. But, I don't really believe that. *(Here he/she starts to cry.)*

(Then why do you teach that?) It is my job and I don't know what else to teach them. In my heart, I feel their life and mine is useless. *(Later, the client said she had sensed that he had gotten into this work because it was the only way he could get out of his humble beginnings.)*

(Do they see through your disbelief?) No, which makes it even more hypocritical in that I am good at deceiving them.

(It must be painful for you?) Yes. Cruel. But, I know not what to do about it. **It is as though I have been cast in a role and the play has already begun and I can't leave the stage.**

(Move to another significant event.) I'm in a church. I'm in my forties. I'm being promoted in the Church. I have on fine garments now versus my monk-like robe. I believe I'm a bishop.

(What are you feeling?) Disbelief! There is so much pomp surrounding the ceremony. I see other men dressed in red—all the same. I'm familiar with the ritual, just not the part I'm playing in it.

(What now?) I'm very powerful. I look older than my forties. Graying hair. This one is fighting this.*(Here our client is fighting the information which she is receiving. She is resisting it.)* I may perhaps even be a Pope. *(One can imagine why she might have resisted this information as this not an everyday*

occurrence.) It is so surprising to me to be a Pope and I don't even believe any of this. Master deceiver that I have risen through this organization. I sense that I don't even believe in an afterlife or God.

(Move to a later time in that lifetime.) I'm conducting Mass. My existence is just going through the motions. No emotions. I don't view it any differently than those peasants in the field. Just a job. They work the fields. I run the Church. To me it is a business.

(What year is it?) 1321.

(What do you do with those who don't agree with your teaching?) I don't get a sense there is much discord. Don't sense I ever experienced that. My job is to make money—to control the finances. That's why I was chosen. Now I'm not even cynical. As the monk, I was torn. Rationalized. Now my job is to run the Church and it's other people's job to teach the philosophy. I'm detached. The people, the Catholics, are just one aspect of the business.

Bettering people's lives through teaching of God is one part—also in real estate, building arms, banking, art and investments.

(Do you enjoy those other aspects?) Yes. I sense that the powers of this organization believe that a secure financial base is important. It's like the spiritual aspects were put on hold while they build this base. Because I have shown I can manage business, I have been selected.

(Do you have any wealth for yourself?) I live well. I'm provided for. I don't skim profits. A nice lifestyle is provided for me.

Alive Again...Again...and Again

Don't sense I was corrupt in any way—just very efficient. It doesn't bother me that this is the focus of my job. Comes to mind that I'd be the perfect CEO of a corporation in today's terms.

(Move to the time preceding your death in that lifetime.) I'm in bed. I'm in my late sixties. I don't look like I've aged much. It's a very elaborate bed and bedroom—a lot of drapery.

(Were there ever any women in your life?) No. Just business.

(No relationships?) I sense none.

(Any emotion?) None. There are men in red robes around. I think they're cardinals.

(Do they show any emotion?) No.

(Move to the time following your death.) They are beginning to prepare the body for viewing—washing me. They're putting on different robes. Apparently I'm to lie in state. They're putting me in white.

(Where is the body?) It's in a church in front of the altar, but toward the aisle. I am in an elaborate coffin on a table. People walk up the aisle and go to the right or to the left. I'm positioned at the end of that aisle. Many people come.

*(What was the lesson you came to learn in that lifetime?) The word that comes to mind is **discretion**. Hardly seems like a lesson. It seems to me looking on it that it was rather an elaborate hoax.*

(Are the people viewing you with love and emotion?) Yes, and I view them with no emotion. It's very odd. It's such a

detached relationship. There is no relationship. I have no feeling whatsoever toward these people.

(I am fascinated at this point because he is commenting on what he is observing after his death, yet not aware that he is aware of what is happening. The most amazing part of this regression was watching him gradually realize that he was observing events that happened after his death. Words cannot describe the emotion that followed that realization.)

(What happens next for you?) I am in the White Light and there are individuals who meet me. I am surprised by this. Recognition is beginning to occur about what is taking place while part of me believes I don't deserve it. (He's emotional at this point.) I'm very sad. I'm sad now because I know I could have given these people more. I want to go back and tell them, but I can't. That is the real lesson. (He cries.)

(Move to that higher level of consciousness that we call the High Self. How is that lifetime impacting the life today?) She has chosen a lifetime of service as we've discussed in the past. She has chosen to become spiritually aware at an early age to impart information to people that may be useful to them. It is in that previous lifetime that he/she became aware of the impact she could have on people. She chose not to. This time she is atoning for that lifetime by becoming spiritually aware and helping others.

*It is a burden to bare that when she had the opportunity to help millions, she did not. Now she has the opportunity to help smaller numbers, but she wants it to be useful. She knows she can deceive. Now she wants to give them what they **need** to hear.*

*As Pope, she/he could deceive to perfection. Could give people what they **wanted** to hear. Now she wants to give people what they **need** to hear. Perfect choice. She wants to help others, but carries around the burden of deceiving them. She has a fear of **winging it.** It is of the utmost importance that the information be accurate for want of a better term. She/He gave out so much that was inaccurate as the Pope. The balance is what is difficult to achieve.*

(What is accurate?) **That the information given and discussed has been important. In regard to accuracy, that is the middle ground—that it is accurate because it is useful.**

It is that other life that makes her so sensitive. If information is not accurate in the traditional sense, it brings up the life of deceit. If it is not accurate, but serves a purpose, it brings up that life. That all that life could have been so deceitful is upsetting—all that energy toward real estate, art, etc. when all those people were looking toward him/her for guidance. Just a tremendous weight because of this. (She cries.)

(At this point we are doing healing work. Sometimes we have discussions with what I call the subconscious mind or we discuss the impact of a particular lifetime at the physical level, emotional level, mental level or spiritual level. In this case we stay at the level of the High Self. We're trying to help this person release the guilt. I remind him that he did not know there was more. I suggested that if he had told them what he truly believed, what would it have done? It would have lead to despair. Would that have served any purpose?) No purpose.

(It seems he suffered more than the people?) Yes. He believed in some strange way that by providing for them a

secure financial position he was helping. Someone else appointed to his position who may have had the **element of grace** could do what he could not. He tried to find it (grace) but he couldn't. (Sobs.) So, he just used his skills to manage the business, never intending to become Pope. At each step he was more and more dismayed.

(Did he try to turn it down?) No. Knowing what the inner circle wanted—financial—he knew he was able to provide that for them. He never discussed his **gracelessness** with them. He didn't turn it down because he knew he could do a good job for them.

(Did someone follow him who had **grace**?) Soon after. It was the second successor. The first successor was still of that group. As they aged, it paved the way for someone who could give the people what they needed.

(What was your name?) John is coming into my head and something with a "P."

(Are you able to forgive him?) Yeah. You're correct, he suffered more than the people. People close to them still gave them what they thought they needed. No new ground was broken in dogma. Sort of maintained a **spiritual status quo**. It's interesting. Something Pontious comes to mind—an **i o u s**.

(Can she in the conscious state forgive him?) Yes. Now that she has seen this life and that there was no intention to deceive. This Pope didn't go out of his way to deceive. It was like a script. He was caught up in a series of events he thought was better to flow with than against.

Much has been discussed. (After this we thank the High

Alive Again...Again...and Again

Self for assistance and ask that healing continue. Blessings are exchanged and I then go through another guided meditation to bring the person back to a normal state of consciousness and ground them.)

Because of the unique perspective on faith, this was an interesting regression. The woman experiencing the regression is one of purity and guilelessness. She has become an outstanding channel but may never publicly acknowledge her gift as she does not seek publicity or wealth. Purity of motivation and information were what concerned her.

The person she was in the regression may have had more in common with people on our planet today than we might care to admit. Have you not met leaders of organizations of power who obviously lacked *grace*? **Because being a recognized leader of an organized religion, business, educational institution or government is a job which often provides prestige, income, housing, retirement benefits and power over others, there is the temptation for people who lack *true grace* to establish themselves as possessors of the knowledge of how others should live their lives and what they should believe.** This can be to manipulate people so that those who have established themselves as the experts can retain their power and prestige. In the regression, the person was despairing because he/she had been so good at fooling the people. Charming and charismatic people are often in these positions. That does not mean that they are genuine. Always look deeper than outward appearances when evaluating the message of another individual or group.

Hopefully the regression points out the danger in letting anyone tell you what you should believe. They may just be

telling you what they think you should know. My client was
concerned that people have the purist, truest information
with which to make their own decisions. You must seek out
good and reliable information and on that make your decisions. With that you are exercising your **will** as when exercising a muscle. **If you do not exercise your will, you will
one day discover that you do not seem to have one.**

As long as you are not involved in practices that hurt
another person, interfere with their free will or harm the
planet, no one knows better what you should believe than
you. In your decision-making process you listen to that small
voice within which comes from your highest level of expression, your High Self or God Self. You listen when you are in
a state of lovingness or peacefulness. You filter out the static
and interference around you and allow yourself time to listen to your inner voice. What conversations these can be!
There is no greater companion or better listener than your
own High Self. Skill must be developed in filtering out the
information that comes from the more physically-oriented
self with its focus on the concerns of the physical world.
Those concerns are important but you have plenty of input
from the physical world. **You are trying to learn to listen to
that part of you which has the broader view.**

This is not to say you should not pay your taxes if you
decide that you believe that paying taxes is not part of your
belief-system. This has more to do with healing your own
mind and learning to use it. The mind is a pure and sacred
place that exists within—and maybe about—each of us and
deserves honor for its own uniqueness. **No two minds will
perceive the same, love the same, think the same, or
believe the same. You must reclaim your power and take
charge of your own mind and your own life. Even lovers**

and parents will try to control your mind. Be *mindful* of who and what is influencing your thoughts. Is it the television to which you have given the power over your mind? Is it a religious leader to whom you have given the power over your mind? Is it a politician to whom you have given the power over your mind? Take that power back!

You will to will what you will in your life. To do that you make decisions. Decisions are made from experience and intrinsic knowledge. Remember this: **You make sense of the world, based on your own experiences** and other information made available to you that is compatible with your personal experience. If you have enough experiences that do not fit what you are told is the way the world is, you either block your own experiences to the contrary or, you re-evaluate your own "philosophy of life." To be told that you are "supposed" to believe a certain way because a majority in a particular culture believes a certain way, creates a bind for the person whose experiences do not support the shared belief system. For those who have had experiences that are "out of the ordinary" or have had awarenesses, even as children, that go beyond the "norm," life can be painful. It is difficult to reconcile these experiences with the prevailing philosophy or paradigm when they just do not fit.

PARADIGM

Paradigm refers to the prevailing philosophy of a culture at a point in time. For example, the culture in which Columbus lived supported the "flat world" theory. Galileo, also, was forbidden by the Church to speak of his theories that the world was round because his theory was not consistent with the teachings of the Church. Scientists, philosophers, and

others on the planet may have shared or even widely accepted the theory of a round world, but, because those people
were not in positions of power and not a large enough group
to exert pressure, they were unable to change the prevailing
paradigms.

**Paradigms are difficult to change, even when there is
evidence to support the change.** Most often, people in positions of power and influence have a vested interest in maintaining the old paradigm. After all, **the old paradigm usually is part of the thinking that supports their position of
power and influence.** For example, through much of this
century, in medicine, the prevailing paradigm was the "germ
theory." People were healthy until a "germ" invaded the
body. We then consulted a doctor to fight the germ. The idea
of a holistic view of health, which included strengenthing the
immune system with attention to proper diet, lifestyle
changes and the use of other healing disciplines such as
acupuncture was ridiculed. Now our culture is moving
toward a holistic view of health—the paradigm is changing,
but not without much struggle against the government and
the medical establishment. **As is often the case, when the
groups in power begin to see that others may take away
some of their power with the new ideas, the former
embrace the "new" ideas as part of their own discipline.
They can then espouse the new paradigm, even if they do
not wholly support it or understand it.**

When my generation was in elementary school, we were
taught that the molecule was the basic building block of the
universe. In high school, we were taught that atoms were the
basic building blocks of the universe. In college, we were
taught about sub-particles, wave theory and vibrations. As
science acquired the instruments to measure minute particles

of matter, our paradigm changed. These major shifts occurred during a rather short period of time. **The universe had not changed, but our tools for measuring its phenomena had become more sophisticated.**

TRUTH

Seeing such changes in "truth" in just a few years, should be impetus enough to explore the unknown and unexplained without restrictive judgements about what is acceptable and what is not. **It is the "unexplained" phenomena, the experiences that do not fit the prevailing paradigm, that provide the clues about where to look for additional knowledge and information.** I'm from Missouri, the "Show Me State." I have always wanted an explanation for everything. Never content to accept an unexplained phenomenon without trying to make some sense of it, I studied philosophy and read everything I could to gain more understanding and make more sense of this world. I learned not to discount my own intuitions, because, more often then not, when I had an intuitive sense about something, I was "right on." Trying always to keep an open mind, I observed and read and listened and thought. How does it all fit? My explorations brought me to the conclusion that there is much that we do not know—and much of it is beyond the physical world as we perceive it. **Hence, the study of metaphysics, or that which is beyond or greater than the physical, became my path. It is my joy and my life.**

This book is about a healing process, which is the result of many years of working with clients through past–life regression and the study of metaphysics. It is certainly not "new" and not unique to me. Many healers and therapists

use similar techniques to help clients make sense of their
world and take charge of their lives by letting go of anger,
resentment, fear, and pain, which restrain them from reach-
ing their potential and achieving joy in their lives. As a
licensed psychotherapist in private practice for several years,
I have worked with clients based on the belief systems they
bring with them to therapy. However, **I am finding a growing number of people who are vitally interested in their
spiritual growth and who feel that addressing spiritual
needs is a significant part of maximizing their potential
and accomplishing a balanced and meaningful life. I do
not use the word spiritual as a synonym for religious.
Spiritual has to do with the connection the individual feels
with their essence and Spirit or God as they perceive God
or Spirit. Religion may or may not support that connection
and is not the subject of this book.**

What may be unique about the book is that the regressions themselves are the focal point. Instead of presenting an
in depth dissertation on a **Western View of Reincarnation**,
or an in–depth analysis of a client's case history, I wanted to
present the stories which are from transcripts of client's
regressions and show how they relate to a particular issue in
the person's present life. This way, perhaps, the reader can
see the usefulness for the regression and see how the stories
might give one insight into one's own life. These regressions
have occurred over a period of time from the 1970's and in
several states. Any attempt to identify the client would be
fruitless as information has been changed to protect his or
her privacy.

The healing process is grounded in the **theory of reincarnation which accepts that there is some aspect of the person
that survives death and is able to move to other planes and**

other dimensions, returning to physical bodies from time to time. This return occurs for the purpose of growth through experiencing physical life in many forms and situations, thus allowing a person to acquire knowledge, which may lead to understanding, which may lead to wisdom. With that process in mind, we can assume that one comes into the physical to learn and to grow. Also, **we might assume that a human being has access to some kind of memory bank which has recorded all the experiences and the reactions to those experiences from all lifetimes. A human being also seems to access another greater source of information which is shared with other human beings so that in an altered state of consciousness, the person knows information which they do not know in the conscious state.**

Regression is the word used to describe the process I and other healers and therapists use to assist clients in understanding more about themselves. **Regression refers to a procedure that takes a person back to the past.** Using a light meditation or hypnosis, one is able to go back to past events or childhood experiences and recall them with clarity. Some clients have been able to recall their birth experiences in detail as well as conversations that occurred during the fetal stage, during birth, and after birth. **Such recall suggests the existence of an intelligence or mind that exists outside the, as yet, unorganized brain of the infant.** That "mind" appears to be able to record the events and to remember the emotions around those events. Evidence suggests that trauma from the birth also seems to impact a person's present life. **What is so surprising is that a therapist can just as easily move a person farther back to time prior to birth—into what we call a "past life!"** When one sees people with diverse educational levels, philosophical backgrounds, and cultures easily slip back into a past life, which helps explain something that is happening in the present, one has to wonder from where the information is coming.

Remember that as a psychotherapist, I also work with clients in the traditional sense and within their own belief system. However, many people in our culture accept reincarnation and want to release any blockages to growth which may have past–life influences. With these people I work differently. They come to me because they have had experiences that are, perhaps, rejected or even ridiculed by other therapists. **Therapists are taught to respect a client's religion or belief system, but, when it comes to metaphysics or psychic phenomena, a few therapists and people think it is acceptable to ridicule the belief system.** Many of these clients are very intuitive and sense that something in their past is unduly influencing their present reactions.

When I begin with a new client, we talk for awhile to determine what issue, or issues, are currently causing them concern. Perhaps, for example, a woman is stuck in a relationship that is harmful to her and from which she does not seem to be able to extricate herself. What is holding her? What is the attraction? What lesson does she need to learn from the experience? I might then guide her through a visualization or a light meditation and then instruct her to go back to another time and place, one that would give her insight into what is happening in her life today. For example, if she is constantly feeling unworthy, or undeserving, I would ask her to go back to the source of those feelings of unworthiness or to another time when she felt unworthy.

Since this book is not intended to be a book on the techniques of regression, I will not present the methods used to take clients to that state of consciousness where access to memories is achieved. I include prayer, protection, and chakra balancing in the procedure. This activity is considered a very spiritual experience and is treated as such.

When in this altered state of consciousness, clients go back to a lifetime in the past that is influencing their present life. As they are questioned, they relate what they are experiencing. Sometimes their experience is very visual, as if they are in a movie. For some, who are less visual, there are "knowings." They just "know," for example, that they are in a stone cottage with a thatched roof and that they are eating a meal with their families. Emotions often manifest during the process. Clients laugh and cry with abandon.

You will notice in the regressions you read that the clients may speak in the first person, the second person or the third person. In the same regression they may even change from one sentence to the next. For example: "I am walking the dog. Oh, he's shot. Someone shot him while he was walking the dog!" The person may be reporting as the person experiencing the action and then become a reporter reporting about the action. The choice may sometimes have to do with how comfortable the person is in the body of that former person. If a traumatic event seems about to occur, I will ask the person to leave the body and be a reporter reporting the event but experiencing no emotion. This is to remove the person from the body to minimize the risk of traumatizing them again with the same event. When we ask a person to move to a higher level of consciousness, to what we call the High Self, the person will most often be referred to as "he" or "she."

How do we explain their ability to go to these past experiences? How do we explain the connectedness to God or to something "greater than" that they describe? **For some there**

is a spiritual experience of such depth that they are over-
come with a joy or a peacefulness they have never known
and cannot explain. Sometimes something is touched—
something far greater than anything the person has ever
experienced in this physical life.

Regression should never be done with clients with mental disorders or those who are suicidal. Past–life work is done
with stable people who want to grow and are interested in
releasing any blockages to that growth. As with any client,
therapists should look first for physical causes of depression
and any other symptoms, and those physical conditions
should be treated by the appropriate persons. Unstable
clients are not candidates for regression work. Also, clients
must be free of mind-altering drugs, including alcohol.

George Santayana in **The Life of Reason** says: "Those
who cannot remember the past are condemned to repeat it."
What is your history? What are the lessons you can learn
from knowing more about your "soul's history"? If we
hypothesize that the soul is eternal and enters many physical
bodies and other forms and dimensions in order to acquire
knowledge and understanding, what can be the value of
knowing some of a soul's "history?" Perhaps lessons on
which a soul is working may become apparent. **Wisdom
might be the result of knowledge from which understanding has been achieved.**

For instance, one may experience a past-life recall, either
through a regression, a clairvoyant awareness of one's own,
or through the awareness of a proven, respected psychic or
channel, and see that similarities exist between one's present
life and the life recalled. These similarities may have to do
with feelings that are aroused or they may have to do with

thought patterns that relate to the issue or theme of the lessons. For example, you have difficulty with intimacy, especially sexual intimacy. When you are involved with someone of the opposite sex, you freeze. You discover that in a past life you were raped or abused by someone you trusted. Your body remembers the pain and your mind remembers the betrayal. Today you have difficulty trusting and being intimate. With understanding—which may be spontaneous or which may take some time and processing—you are able to "work through" the problem and, hopefully, to master it.

WORKING THROUGH

"Working through" is a phrase often used to refer to the process of resolving pain, guilt, fear, and other conditions including emotions or thought patterns, that are stored in the memory bank to which I referred earlier. This memory bank is your computer and those emotions or thought patterns stored there may or may not be based on correct or pertinent information. "Old tapes" refers to recurring, outdated, no longer useful patterns of thinking and feeling. They are like an old record or tape that "goes on " automatically. Some "old tapes," which might be playing, may actually be primitive in that they relate to lives during the times of cave dwellers when you had to appear to be ferocious to earn the respect of the wild beasts or other threatening members of your own species. Grunting as a form of communication may have been acceptable then but is less acceptable today. You might determine from this example that you have some work to do on communication skills. This may be a silly example but you get the point. In other words, you might find yourself overreacting to stimuli in your life, or worrying about dangers that do not exist, or experiencing pain where no physical source is determined. In later chapters, the concept of "old tapes" and how those tapes could be affecting your present life will be further explored.

Letting Go

Another term often used in today's therapy and self-help climate is "letting go." **We have "let go" when we are no longer affected by an experience.** This act is a valuable and necessary step on the road to healing. What often happens, however, is a push by therapists, friends, and family members to a "premature letting go." It is all well and good to let go of pain, anger, resentment, etc.; but if the purpose for the experiences in a lifetime is to acquire knowledge and understanding, why would you let go of something before you have gained at least some understanding about what and why it happened? Those who are grieving the loss of loved ones, of health, of possessions, of anything else, are often admonished to "get on with your life." "Put the past behind you." If you "let go" prematurely and have not properly "worked through" the grieving process, every time a similar situation occurs such as a loss for someone else, your old "issues," or feelings around grief and loss surface, demanding attention. If you continue to "stuff" them, or ignore them, they'll fester under the surface. **It is as if the pain is always present inside, and there is a certain quantity of it and it must be released.** Even if you are just working with present-life material, you will sense the need to understand where you have been and why, and where you want to go in the future and how you can avoid some of the same obstacles.

A wise old teacher of mine once used the example of

someone driving down the road in an automobile that went around a bend in the road and hit a brick wall. Ouch! The driver says, "I'm not going to do that again." Later, he is coming down the same road, but he is in a hurry to get to his destination. He knows there is danger somewhere along this path, but thinks he can swerve to miss it and, just when he was making really good time, crashes again. After a period of healing our driver again starts down the road. This time he travels a little slower because he remembers there are some hazards along this path.

Sometimes when a person is traumatized from a crash or something like that, he is confused and does not necessarily remember clearly what happened to him. He sometimes forgets the dangers after time passes. The next time he notices the signs along the way, such as "entering treacherous roadway," "beware of potholes in the road," and "watch for obstruction in the road." Rounding a blind corner, he again hits the brick wall, but only slightly, because he was going slowly enough to swerve. The damage is slight. Later, he again travels that road, but this time he drives carefully and looks for the signs. When he sees the signs he adjusts his behavior accordingly and manages to avoid another collision. So it is with life or "lives." By looking back over past experiences, you begin to see the signs. You see the advantage of traveling a little more slowly so you can be aware of the road conditions along the way. You might even decide that is not the road you want to take after all.

KNOW THYSELF

We seem to be called to examine our lives. We heard the phrase, "Know Thyself," repeated for centuries. Live the examined life. Learn from your experiences and the experiences of those around you. Learn from your own past experiences. A teacher for whom I had great respect, Dr. Mary Lill Lee Colvin, often used a phrase I loved: "It's all grist for the mill." In other words, **all the grain or experiences you bring to the mill of life are for the product that will ultimately come through that mill. None are wasted.**

Many past-life stories are presented in the chapters that follow. Explanations of the possible therapeutic benefits of past-life regression are presented. If you can gain understanding of your own issues because of some similarities to the situations presented, then the purpose of this book has been fulfilled. This work has been done with sincerity and love. It is a gift to others "on the path" who may feel alone and not understood by their loved ones or communities. Family members and friends are not always the most supportive when you venture away from the "accepted" paradigm. Just know that some of the greatest minds throughout history have dared to believe differently than the majority, and those are the people who made a difference in our history. **Sometimes it is frightening to be different from others, but even more frightening is to lose the "self" in order to be accepted.** Remember Polonius' speech to his son, Laertes, in Shakespeare's **Hamlet** in which he says:

> *This above all, to thine own self be true,*
> *And it must follow as the night the day*
> *Thou canst not then be false to any man.*

I can no more change my beliefs because someone tells me I should, than I can change the color of my skin or my height or anything else that is natural or unique to me. If the experiences of my life support a way of believing that is different from others, then so be it.

Of course, you are not expected to believe in reincarnation or past-life regression in order to benefit from this material. You might look at this book as an exploration of possibilities. Also, you might look at this book as a way to acquire information and understanding about a topic that may be of interest to some of your family and friends. Wanting to treat them with respect and sensitivity, you keep an open mind.

Chapter I

What Is A Regression?

A regression is a peek into a soul's history. The events are significant enough to be recalled while in an altered state of consciousness. **Because many believe some of the events of the past are impacting present lives, regressions can be a useful tool for understanding issues in the present life and healing issues which may be troublesome.** Whether or not past lives exist at all or are just some elaborate creation of the mind, is not known. What we do know is that these elaborate creations of the mind may seem to have an amazing healing effect on individuals who are seeking insight into such issues as relationships, phobias, allergies, physical pains, fears and thought patterns that they wish to change.

There is no proof that the regressions presented in this book are past lives, but I can share with you my experience of more than ten years of work with regressions. Nearly everyone who comes to me for a regression, whether or not they believe they even have past lives, seems to go, with very little effort, to some other time and place and gives a detailed account of what they are experiencing. They cry when their baby or mate dies. They get angry at injustices they have seen. They glow from the peaceful times when life was very simple. **In fact, one of the first things I do with depressed people, after we have determined the physical status of the depression, is take a person who may never have experienced joy or love in the present lifetime to one in which they knew great joy. This, then, becomes a memory they own and a reference point for joy or love.**

We mentioned thought patterns which a person may want to change. **Thought patterns are like automatic tapes which run through your head and color your perceptions of the world about you.** They are thoughts that repeat themselves like a message played from a tape. Preserving and presenting those "automatic tapes" seems to be a function of the subconscious mind. Examples of common tapes are: "I can't do anything right," "I'm not worthy of success or of having good things happen to me," "I'm a failure." "If I ever achieve anything—happiness or wealth—it will just be taken away, so why try," and many others. **The subconscious mind is the "keeper of the tapes." Those tapes can affect the individual on one or more levels—the physical, the emotional, the mental or the spiritual.**

WORTHINESS

Lack of worthiness or not deserving, for some mysterious reason, is a common tape or theme for many individuals. Even though they have lived a life in which they never intentionally hurt another person and acted from a place of sincere intent to do the best that they could, they are haunted by some sense of not deserving any better than they are getting or even not deserving what they are getting. That kind of perception of the self can help sabotage the best efforts. It would need to be changed. The regression which follows is an example of a truly sincere individual who has a highly developed sense of justice and would never hurt another human being. Yet, she has had the feeling of deserving to be persecuted because she is not worthy of any better. There is no logical foundation for the perception of unworthiness so we took her to an altered state of consciousness and asked to be shown a lifetime where such a thought pattern may have developed. Her story follows, and, we may add, it was related with great emotion.

(Describe the vegetation along the path.) There's brown, dead grass with patches of snow and some trees in the distance. There's a little house, some of it is logs and some of it is wood. Someone has painted some flowers around the door. It's dark inside. There are small windows that don't let in much light. There's a table and benches. My family is there. I'm female, I guess. I'm in my teens— about fourteen or fifteen. Mother and father are there, some brothers, a small sister and my aunt.

(Go to the time of the main meal.) Potatoes again and some cabbage, some beets, some pickles and some bread are the meal. It's that same thing we have all the time. (This was said in a disgusting tone of voice.)

(Later.) There seems to be a gathering of the people in the village. It's mostly the men. The women stand around the edges. Everybody is angry and upset—something

about what the government is telling them today. I don't understand. I don't care. My friends and I are talking.

(Later.) We're having to leave our home. It's not a good place to be anymore. We're packing everything up on a cart. Others are also leaving. We're trying to all travel together. My mother is sick. She's having another baby and she's sick. We had to stop for awhile. They gave us some blankets to put up on the trees. It's so cold. My aunt is crying. We're putting all the blankets on my mother to keep her warm. I'm trying to fix food for everybody. It's hard— hard to keep the fire going. My father's going off to find some help. Little kids are crying. Everybody's upset.

(Later.) My mother died. And, the baby died. My father didn't come back. I don't know what we're going to do.

(Who's with you?) There's my aunt, two older brothers, little sister and little brother. One brother isn't well. All he does is read. He doesn't do very much. He keeps crying. We load up the wagon and take my mother's body and the baby. We won't leave them there. I don't know where to go. Why is this happening to us? What did we do?

(Did father leave any money or anything?) We didn't have any money—just animals. There were two cows and some chickens. We have to travel when it is dark. There are bad people out there. They are trying to hurt us. My brother says they killed my father.

(Later.) My aunt is sick, too. All she does is cry. She doesn't like my mother's body with us. I like having it with us. It makes me feel good. She helps take care of us. (Sighing.) I'm so tired. I'm so scared. Some people from the

village have come back to help us. They are taking us with them. They buried my mother and the baby. Now we have to hurry away. They don't know what happened to father. They just found his body. He'd been beaten. They say we can go on a long, long journey away and be safe. It's not good where we are—not safe. It's another village. I miss my mother and father. I'm so scared. We're all so scared. I want to help but I don't know what to do. My aunt and I fight all the time. I want her to be like my mother, but she's so scared. We're traveling pretty fast. We have to stay away from the villages so we go way out into the country.

(Later.) Oh, oh, oh. They're coming. They're coming after us. They killed our cow. I'm trying to hide my brother and sister. They're a bunch of men. They're having a good time. Drinking. Kicking us. I can't save them. They killed my aunt and my brother. They take me. I've never seen my other brother and sister again. Don't know what happened. I felt it was my fault they were hurt.

(Why?) Because I was the one the family left to take care of them. The others were busy with their own families, their own business. They just let us travel with them. Many were killed. They took everything of value and hurt the men so they couldn't do much. They raped some of the women and took us younger ones with them.

The men were from some village not far from where we camped. **They hated us. They hated us and they don't even know us.** *They made me a servant in their house—a man and his son. They would kick me all the time. They would rape me all the time. I tried to run away a couple of times to find out what happened to my family—my friends. They wouldn't let me get very far. I'm eighteen.*

Alive Again...Again...and Again

(Later.) I'm dying. I'm still very young. Eighteen. I'm having a baby, but things aren't right. I'm hurting all the time and bleeding all the time. I don't want to have this baby. It's time to go.

(Have you been shown any kindness through this?) Not much. None of the women in the family liked me very much. They didn't think I did things well enough. I slept on the floor—always far away from the fire, sometimes outside in the barn with the animals. They're angry with me that I'm having a baby. It makes them realize what the men have been doing. It makes them face it. They'll blame me, though. They'll blame me.

(Preceding death.) I'm having the baby. A lot of blood. Oh, so much blood. I'm just bleeding to death. I had a little boy. They took him away from me. I wanted him. It was something to love. I just live a few more hours. The baby's okay. He lives with these people.

(Do you see the body?) Yes. It's in the house on a blanket on the floor. They're mad at me because I made such a mess. All that blood. They're sorry to see me go, though, because they won't have anyone to do the work. One of the men, not the father of the baby, the young man, is sorry to see me go. He's sad, but he doesn't say anything.

(What did you learn from that lifetime?) I don't know that I learned very much. I suffered all the years after I lost my family. **I felt I failed them and didn't deserve any better than I got.** *I couldn't save my mother or my aunt. I couldn't protect my brother and sister. I didn't learn. I just survived till I died.*

Alive Again...Again...and Again

(I'm moving you to a higher level of consciousness—to what we call the High Self.)

(Physical level—Is there trauma at the physical level?) Yes. There's been a lot of impact. Just one of many lifetimes that have impacted this body.

(Is the physical body ready to release the memory?) No. She must want to release. There's still some wanting to hold on.

(Emotional level—Is there trauma at the emotional level?) Much impact. There is low self-esteem and blaming herself for her problems. There's a sense of not having done what she should have done.

(Mental level—Are there thought patterns affecting her life today?) Yes. Negative thought patterns. Feelings of not deserving.

(Spiritual level—Any impact at the spiritual level?) Not too much impact.

(I'm moving you to another level of consciousness—to what we call the subconscious mind.)

(I must compliment the subconscious mind on it's attempts at preventing this kind of pain from happening again. Is she ready to release those memories now?) Yes. It is time.

(Physical level—Ready to release cellular memory?) Yes. It's a start. Some hesitation, but yes.

*(What purpose is the physical pain serving?) It is part-
ly, also, to help ground her—to keep her in the physical.*

*[Please note that ground refers to the condition of
being fully in the physical or of this physical world in contrast to being disconnected or spaced-out, as we often say.
Many who can reach higher levels of consciousness lessen
contact with their physical selves. Pain reminds the person of the "physical-ness" of their earth experience.
Ideally, one wants to be connected to and open to the spiritual self or High-Self while keeping the feet firmly on the
ground. I often refer to those who have lost much of their
connection as "space cadets." Grounding is an important
part of this work.]*

*(Emotional level—Willing to release?) Yes. (We
worked on releasing the emotional pain associated with
those memories.)*

*(Mental level—May we work on the thought patterns
at this time?) Yes.*

*(Is it logical to think that a fourteen-year-old girl could
save her family under the conditions existing in that lifetime?) No.*

(Can she release that assumption at this time?) Yes.

*(Can it be replaced with an acceptance that she did the
very best that she could do under the circumstances and
that nothing she could have done at that time could have
saved the family from the course that was developing?) Yes,
and she forgives herself for the years of beating herself up.
Must forgive herself.*

Alive Again...Again...and Again

(Can she forgive that family that was so cruel?) Yes.

(High Self — Return now to that higher level of consciousness.)

(Was she Jewish?) Yes, it was a Jewish lifetime—about 200 years ago. It was in what is part of Poland, Germany and Austria. They were sent from that district. **There was not an order to kill them but, as always happens, (such an order) stirs up some people who have hatred. They take out their fury on others and call it justice.**

(Was there a precipitating event?) The Jews were beginning to be prosperous. They had successful farming ventures and people wanted their land. A very common story.

(Is she able to release the need to be persecuted?) She's working on it. She's working on it in many ways. This is a big help to her. She always felt she deserved any misfortune that came her way—set herself up for many problems. It's a hard way. **She chose to learn her lessons in this way. It gives her compassion and empathy for people in trouble. She has a strong, strong feeling for justice and for how governments hurt people.**

LEVELS OF CONSCIOUSNESS

Several of the concepts present in this regression will be discussed in later chapters. For instance, the concept of the High Self may be new to many. **For now, think of it as the highest level of consciousness you can reach. Think of the subconscious mind as a lower level of consciousness that is the programming or recording aspect of consciousness—**

the "automatic tapes"—which lacks the analytical capabil-
ity of other levels. Clients report that they can feel the shift
in consciousness between the subconscious and the High
Self. There is a sense of "wiseness" or "all-knowingness"
with the High Self. Physical, emotional, mental and spiritual levels of being are used to refer to parts of the self
which, though actually part of the whole and coexisting,
serve specialized functions. By addressing those specialized functions, we discover the impact of specific experiences on that particular function and initiate change. In
other words, we try to influence the automatic programming affecting that particular function.

In the regression above, we accessed the experience by
asking for the source of the thought pattern. Though the
thought pattern or mental level of functioning was the primary recorder of that experience, the other levels—physical,
emotional and spiritual—were also affected, more or less.

RELATIONSHIPS

Another client was concerned because relationships
never lasted and she was having difficulty knowing how
bold or self-expressive she should be at work and in relationships. Two regressions were experienced which seemed
to be lessons in boldness and how to temper it with some
caution without giving up the self. Words alone could not
explain the subtleties that were understood from the example of these two lifetimes. Pay particular attention to how
both sides of the same issue were presented.

> (You are on a path. Describe the vegetation around
> you.) It's just green, like ground cover.

Alive Again...Again...and Again

(The path will take you to the place where you live. What do you see?) I see a mansion like in the South with porches. It's light. There's no furniture in the entrance. There are stairways and a view through the house. There's a dining room and a table. It's very formal. They're just starting to serve. I'm male and I'm twenty-eight. I'm sitting on one of the sides toward the head. There's about five people. My father is at the head. He's fearsome, but not cruel. He's in charge. So, I'm kind of like, *(hesitates for awhile)* I don't have as much power as I'd like. There are a couple of women. One's a sister and I don't know the other. There's no wife and a maid is serving the meal.

(Later.) I'm outside and I'm the same age. I'm at some kind of fair or outside fair. I have a friend with me, a guy. We're just looking for fun. We're flirting. I saw myself getting on some kind of horse and showing off. There are women there. I don't get much feeling for them. I don't think of them that much. What I'm really interested in, in that life, is the work issue. I want more power and respect—not to be put down. Looks like it's going to be a long time. Father has some respect and he'll use me, but he won't give up the power. He reminds me of my boss (her present boss). Feel like I'm never going to do anything—just wait. Like Prince Charles. Stuck. It's the family business. I don't have a career. I feel like I'm just wasting away and not doing anything productive.

(Couldn't you move to another place?) In those days you didn't go anywhere. It's not so awful to go away.

(Later.) I'm older, about thirty-eight or so. I think I'm married and have a child.

(Is the wife significant?) No. Maybe. Not the issue. Not what I think about. I feel like I moved away to set up some kind of business. I guess I'm doing alright. It's not on a grand scale like my father's. I still feel threatened by my father. He resents it that I moved away. He doesn't want me to succeed. He would undermine me. I still want the position of my house that I lived in before. I feel banished though I did it myself.

(Later.) I think I'm inside. I'm older, about ten years or so. I'm in some type of building where accounting gets done over an establishment that produces something like a grainery.

(Your business?) No. I'm there doing business with them. I think I sell things to them—a product from the land like grain or something. It feels like I'm in financial trouble. There's this feeling of being a failure—not a big failure like bankrupt.

(Later.) It's Christmas time. It's inside and there's kids playing. It's cheerful. I'm kind of old. I'm sitting on the couch. This is my family. They're happy and I like them. They all think the house is good, and a success and they're in a good family. I think they're wrong thinking this is good. They don't realize. I still feel like a failure. It's not the house my father had. Don't know what happened to that. Business was not that good. It got comfortable. I don't think they have high enough standards when I see these kids laughing.

(Preceding death.) I'm on a bed. I'm real old. I have a bald head. I'm being taken care of by my daughter. There are other women around. I don't feel like a heavy-duty

failure—just want out. No fun. I don't feel emotionally connected to anyone. I don't abuse them. I like them. I just feel like the sooner I'm out the better because it hasn't worked out.

(Following the death.) I'm just looking down on the body. I feel like I didn't take enough chances—wasn't bold enough. I tried everything, but I was never bold enough.

(Lesson?) **To be bold. Think independent. Make my own way without caring what others thought, like my father.** *There was a lack of self-esteem. I was supposed to have had some fun. But, instead, I was just waiting it out.*

(Move to a higher level of consciousness, to what we call the High Self.)

(How is that life impacting the life today?) Through a belief that it can't work out if try something wholehearted-ly. That there's only a level of mediocrity available. Through a fear of living fully.

(Is it affecting the career and love-life?) It affects her career. It affects the feeling that **other people can succeed and there's only a certain level available to me.**

(Is that thought-pattern rooted in another past life?) Yes.

(Go to another time when you felt things wouldn't work out if you tried something wholeheartedly.) Too hard. (Hesitates.) Maybe.

(Where are you?) I'm outside. I think it's some kind of

Alive Again...Again...and Again

*jungle. There are heavy weeds or something. It's green. I'm
a boy, I think. It's like a more primitive time. I'm a person
in a tribe. A teenager.*

*(Where are you going?) Well, I'm going to the village,
alone. I think things are going on in the village. There's some
kind of commotion. We're not being attacked—it's an emotional commotion. It's not a big village. There are just a few
huts. Something has happened. I think it was something dis-
honest—group got stolen from. Whoever did it isn't there.
They're just discovering it. Maybe I know something, but
I'm not guilty. Maybe a friend or someone I trusted may
have done it. I feel a little bit guilty, but I didn't know it. I
may have helped him without knowing it.*

*(How do they react to you?) They don't react to me.
They don't know anything. I didn't know. Afterwards I fig-
ured it out. I don't say anything; it wouldn't help.*

*(Later.) I'm outside in front of a lake. I threw rocks into
the water. I'm with a girl. I'm real friendly with her. We're
about eighteen. We're flirting with each other. We just walk
into the water and play.*

*(Later.) I'm older. It's like the time to make big decisions.
The men in the tribe—there's arguing. Different factions
want control and I'm one of the leaders. I get mad and I'm
arguing. I think I just quit and leave. **Someone stabbed me
in the back when I leave.** It's not fatal. It's a surprise. In
those days that was not considered as horrible to do that. I
was like in shame. I was supposed to leave because I was
causing trouble. I'm not real badly hurt. It's more like being
banished again. Huh! (She pauses, having made a connection to similar feelings from the life presented earlier.)*

Alive Again...Again...and Again

*(What happened next?) I just left. I don't know where I went. I don't think I was married. I think I went some-place and wasn't always alone. I was never accepted by another tribe. They would let others come, but never accepted. I couldn't be part of the power. I never felt like I could. I survived—just killing time. I had no roots. **I had no way to go back and make it okay.***

(Preceding death.) I'm outside in the field alone. It's a sudden death. I'm about fifty-eight. I think I did have a wife and child in the tribe, but I never saw them. I think I might have been hit by a rock, maybe an arrow. It was not personal. It was more like a stranger killed me. I died in the field and nobody was around.

*(Lesson?) **To blend with people. To be a part of the way things run in a group. I think I had supposed to have been a leader and it didn't work out.***

(Move to that higher level of consciousness, the High Self.)

(Was she bold?) Yes.

(And it failed?) Yes.

*(Is there a fear of being bold?) **That and failure and fear of being banished, of never getting back. Regrouping.***

(How affecting present life?) She still is afraid to be bold. She had tried. As a child she tried and the same kinds of things happened. Now she wants to be bold. Same thing happening at work. She still cares too much about how

others see her. She's afraid to leave that perception and go into her own perception. There's a lot of fear.

Maybe there should be a lesson in certain kinds of caution. Be bold and still be part of a group. Boldness should not be failure. That's the main thing—to not hold herself back all the time. The failure comes from not being bold.

(Relationships, too?) Same dynamic. Fear of being self—self esteem, because of the fear of being alone. Not going wholeheartedly gives same results. High Self on the side of being bold. Does not guarantee results. Says must try again. Lose if don't and at least have a chance if try.

(Is this a subconscious tape?) Yes. There's a belief, that **if you do something wholeheartedly, nothing will come of it. They will banish you if you rebel against their power and try to change something.**

(Worked on convincing the subconscious to allow some boldness. It finally agreed—partially.) Okay, but be careful. But, what if she gives up things like jobs? Don't know if you could trust that. (Couldn't completely convince the subconscious to let go of the old tapes.)

(Will the subconscious allow more boldness?) Something accomplished.

(Relationships, too?) Yes.

(Must be herself?) Yes. It's not that far out of her grasp and it won't take that long.

Alive Again...Again...and Again

CHANGING TAPES

Remember, the subconscious thinks it is protecting you by sticking to the old tapes because the tapes were based on experience. It does not always see that a situation may be different in another lifetime. Changing the programming> of the subconscious is not easy, nor should it be. There must be some positive thought pattern to take its place. When I was working on changing the tapes, I would ask the subconscious questions like, "Is it possible the situation is different this time, that she would not be banished?" or point out that in this culture one is not stabbed and banished for disagreeing with leadership. **The subconscious has to be convinced. If it is not the ally for the person trying to change old thought patterns, it will sabotage efforts to make change until it is convinced. That is its job.**

Six months later this client returned looking for more insight into career issues. Her statements included: "Why can't I get to that next level? I know I'm good. What do I have to learn from this?" With those statements as the key, we asked for a regression that would give us insight into what is happening at work today. Pay attention to how this relates to and is another dimension of the same issue—boldness— previously discussed. **How bold can you be in presenting your convictions without being banished and at what point do you modify or let go of those convictions?** The distinctions are very subtle and this story gives more insight into those subtleties than would verbal discussion.

(What is the vegetation like along the path?) There are wildflowers, tall weeds, wildflowers that are purple. I see a village—a renaissance type village.

(Describe your dwelling.) It's tudor style. There are streets going in all directions. My house is on the corner. There's a dark and heavy wood door. Outside is stucco that is white. It's right on the street. There's no front yard. It's a dark hallway. We're supposed to go upstairs. There's not much downstairs. There are two rooms; the left is where you eat and the right is the bedroom. There's a wooden table and there's a woman who's serving. I think there are children. I think I'm a man. She's serving. I think there are two or three children. There may be a wife and a serving girl—I'm not sure.

(Later.) There's something to do with horses. They're trying to get away or stampede. I'm trying to keep them calm. Some are mine and some are others. They're in like a public place and they're getting out of control. They're on the street and they're hooked up, but they're reacting to something. I have a sense of responsibility. I'm supposed to keep them under control. They're hooked to some kind of metal sheet. They're wilder than they are supposed to be. They are out of control.

I do get them calm. My partners are there. They are angry about it. It's a botch-up. Even if they're calm, they are still not right. I think I might have bought them or went someplace and judged them myself and brought them in. I thought they were good horses. I still think so, but maybe not together. I didn't pick the mildest horses on purpose. I wanted them to have spirit. Maybe when they are separated, they will be okay. I think there are a couple of partners and some people who expect some horses. There are more people involved.

(Later.) I'm in some kind of tavern with someone.

Alive Again...Again...and Again

We're drinking beer or ale. I'm talking to him. I feel sure that we're discussing it. He needs convincing. I feel sure it's going to work out. Those horses didn't entirely work out. There were some glitches. I'm telling him my way of judging is still good.

(Later.) Well, I think I'm by a stream with a horse. It's a beautiful day and a beautiful horse. I liked it. Then I got on the horse bareback. It had a harness in it's mouth. There are other people coming up behind me along the river. I don't know if they're threatening or not. They broke the mood. They're official or on business and we were just playing around. They stop a bit and then they go by. I feel like the Lone Ranger—like **my attitudes are my attitudes and not many others share them.**

(Later.) I think it's some kind of wedding. People are dancing. We're clapping our hands. It's like folk dancing. I'm standing in the shade by a booth. It's real relaxing. I don't feel a lot of connection with people in this life. I think I like the children. I don't really focus on the wife. She seems to have a small brain. She's not concerned about issues, not smart. The children aren't even concerned that much. They seem like her children. I have a real passion for horses and what they stand for. There are two kinds—mild and spirited. My thing seems to be to promote the wild ones. I must be a horse trader. I don't own them. I deal with them and I judge them. That one horse may have been mine.

(Later.) I seem to be having an argument with someone who has retained my services. He's out of control. He does not like my horses or something. He's an influential customer so this is very serious. He's a businessman. He does not get tangled up with wild or mild. He'd rather have a

mixture. It's easier to deal with. He's more pragmatic. I think he's my boss now (in the present life). His opinion is practical, but like a sellout. He would turn on me if his clients weren't happy. He goes with the wind.

(Is there not some value to his opinions?) Yes, but I feel if I don't promote the wild horses, the best will die out. It's a moral issue.

(Are you flexible?) He's not bending and I don't think I am either. I don't want the mild horses. It's like the mild ones are brown and the wild ones are black. **It's like mediocrity will take over. The black one, the wild ones, are the creative and the other are mediocre. I can see the same issue at work** (in the present life).

(Are you out of a job?) Yes. I think so. He's trying to compromise. He'll take a couple. Now, I have all these wild horses. Career-wise, I don't know what I'll do with all these horses. I may have to travel with them.

(Later.) This is weird. I have my family with me and we're traveling. We're moving like a gypsy caravan.

(Are there many of you?) There's not that many. It doesn't seem like enough to start a business. Maybe I go to a town and become a blacksmith or see if things are different there. We're pretty close. We all go together. The children are fairly small.

(Later.) It's a much quieter town, less like a city. It's more primitive and less bustling. Seems like there's straw on some of the roofs. I don't think it's that uncommon for people to travel into towns. It's not that long a trip. They're *pretty friendly; it's comfortable there. There's not a lot of strain like the other town. It's poorer. I don't deal in horses much. I'll have to do something else. I don't know what I'll do yet.* **I will let the horse issue go by. I got tired of that battle.**

(Later.) I'm a blacksmith there. My house is like right next door to my shop. I'm busy. I know what to do. I know horses. People come to me. There's another blacksmith, but that's okay. I think I'm better. I like it here. They're friendly. I have friends and I feel important to the town. I'm not arrogant, but a good addition. It's real comfortable. It's not like the big time, but I like it there.

(Preceding death.) I'm maybe fifty-two. I'm on a bed and I'm sick. My wife is putting hot compresses on my head. She's praying. The sun is out. It's a nice day, but I'm dying. Sick. It's a fever or something. I'm not gloomy.

(Following the death.) Now I'm outside the body looking at the cottage. It's a small cottage. I'm looking down at the wife. The children are not there. She's sad. I think it's silly for her to be sad, but I'm out. I look at the house and the wife and it seems so small. **When you are out of the body, you feel like such a big spirit and the other seems so small.**

(Go to a higher level of consciousness, to what we call the High Self.)

(What was the lesson?) **That it was important to fight and have convictions, and it's okay to drop them. It's important to have passions, but also okay to detach from them and live at a different level.**

Alive Again...Again...and Again

That's not selling out. *That was a good life.*

(What is the lesson in the present life?) She doesn't want to hear that yet. She doesn't want to give up fighting. She doesn't see the value yet. There are parallels. There's the issue of what the boss wants and appreciates in her— the more day to day, just get the job done, do what the clients want and don't go for the more creative expression. So, the choice would be to either leave that job and do something else. Or . . . I don't think you can give up the fight unless you give it up all together.

(Like the blacksmith she could move to a job of just being a technician?) She thinks that's the choice.

(Is that the choice or can it be different this time?) No. That's not the choice. The battle can be won, but at a more detached level. Not the passions. ***The arguing is different from the creativity. There has to be detachment in the arguing. Creativity has to be more for itself and not the issue.***
(Do you mean not to take it personally?) Yes. In that lifetime it appeared to be the only choice. In this lifetime, the fight is not the most holy goal. Detachment is, and kindness.

(Will she need to leave her present company to do this?) She can practice in her present job and is practicing. The present job is like the old city. She needs a purer environment. She has to get rid of the tendency because it wouldn't be acceptable there (at the new job). They're beyond that. Otherwise she would go to another job and things wouldn't be any better.

You can see with the above regression that she is still struggling with changing some "old tapes" and clarifying her options around boldness and self-expression by understanding the lessons that can be learned from the situation in which she finds herself.

PAIN AS A KEY

In the earlier regressions we accessed the material through thought patterns. Another way to access material is through physical sensations, pain or body markings such as birthmarks. Though the memory of the event is presenting itself through some kind of physical awareness, when we access the experience, we will usually find a strong emotional and/or mental impact as well. **Physical discomfort was the key.** In the regression which follows, pain in the side was the key used to access the experience which might be the source of the physical pain. However, in addition to physical pain, the experience revealed great emotional pain around the issue of self-esteem. Because of an accident which caused the pain in the side, the person was unable to earn a living and the self-esteem was affected because he could no longer practice his profession. At the time of the session, the client was considering a career change.

> (Describe the vegetation along the path.) I can't see any vegetation. It's rocky. I have on boots. I'm a male and twenty-five years old. There's a two-story house with stairs going up and it's made of some kind of stucco. There are brighter colored door and window sashes. There are no lights but light is coming through the windows. There's a table, soup, and someone else is there who is female and older. Perhaps it is my mother. Her energy is not familiar.

(Later.) We're at a fair—someone else and I. She's female and more my age. I'm getting engaged. She's familiar (in the present life). There are rides and we're on the merry-go-round. We're laughing and in love.

(Later.) She has a baby in her arms and I'm getting ready to leave for work. I'm happy. I have a shovel and ropes and a bucket. There's a lot of dirt. We walk to work. We're digging wells.

(Later.) I have on a white shirt with my sleeves rolled up and I'm wearing a leather apron and I'm pounding with a mallet. Shoes. I've changed jobs, I'm forty-two, I have four children and I make and repair shoes.

(Later.) I'm going someplace in a cart. It's wooden. Ireland. Someone's with me. A horse is pulling the cart. It has a bench, a wooden bench. I'm taking somebody someplace, a family member, my wife. We're going to her mother's. It's a good marriage.

(Later.) We're burying somebody. My mother. She's in a box. She was sixty years old. My wife is not there. I don't remember the father.

(Later.) I'm back at work. I enjoy the work. My son's coming to see me to show off something new. We're going for a ride. It's a new cart. We're close. He's proud of it. We talk some, he's excited. He's twenty-three. We're going through the trees to the country to his farm. It's kind of rainy and muddy.

(Doesn't that make the trip a little more treacherous?) Uh huh.

Alive Again...Again...and Again

(Have you arrived yet?) No. We're bouncing around. There are rocks. There's another cart meeting us on the road. The horses collide, we tip and I fall out. And, the cart falls and the horses rear back. My son falls out, but the other cart doesn't fall over. My son is hurt some. The cart falls on me and I can't get up. I'm old. I'm lying on my side and my legs are doubled up beneath me. I have broken bones. It's my arm I use to make shoes. I'm holding it at the elbow. My ribs are broken. My collar bone is broken. It's the right side from the waist up—the elbow, ribs and collar bone. I can hold it with the other hand. We're going to get into the cart and take me to a doctor. We have to get the horse hooked back up. The other cart owner is going to help. There's a cover on the cart. I'm going to lie down. **I can't make shoes anymore.** *(There was much emotion in this statement.)*

(Won't the arm heal?) I'll try but it won't be the same. I can only fix now, maybe.

(Later.) I don't work anymore. And, I walk with the arm held up even with my waist. I move from my rocking chair to the kitchen. I like it by the fire. My wife likes to go out. She goes by herself during the day. She sews. I feel bad, I can't work. I don't have a shop anymore. I'm getting old, but my wife is spry. She brings in money sewing. Our family comes. We saved money. They (the son and his family) come to visit, but not too often. They come to show off their babies. He feels badly about what happened. I don't blame him. I can't work. I'm proud. I can't make shoes anymore. I play with the children when they come, but they don't come often. **I'm ashamed.**

(Even though it is not you fault?) I can't make a living.

Alive Again...Again...and Again

(Is that the measure of a man?) At that point it is. I don't want to be here.

(Later.) I'm going to my bed. I'm 65 years old. I haven't been ill. Just moving. Get into bed. I don't move too fast. I don't need to be here anymore. My wife, she comes to bed. She turns to her side and goes to sleep and I still think. She makes nice quilts—we have one on the bed. She doesn't need me.

(Death.) My children are around and my wife. I'm still in bed. I didn't get up. I didn't need to be there. She's crying and upset. She didn't understand.

(What was the lesson you came to learn?) To be useful, to be supportive, and not to stand in people's way.

(Was there another time when you did not feel useful— another lifetime?) Yes.

(Go to a higher level of consciousness—to what we call the High Self.)

(How has this affected the right side?) I can't feel bad if I don't work.

(Do you feel you must work all the time?) No.

(Are the massage treatments helping?) Yes. [This client was having massage treatments to help with the pain that had developed.]

(Will the right side release the trauma?) Yes.

(What can we do now?) Just be supportive. It will go away. I couldn't make shoes.

(But it's okay now?) Yes.

Did the contemplation of a career change stir up or bring up the old fear of making a living? Was the pain to be a reminder of the danger of not doing what you normally do to make a living? **There is a sense that often pain is a clue to some kind of past trauma that is influencing the present life.** Occasionally I have had a person place their hand over an area where there is discomfort and allow the memory to come into focus. This is usually done only when other accessing methods are not working, though that is not to say it is a lesser method of access.

WORLD WAR II VETERAN

One young woman had abdominal pain that she had experienced most of her life. Medical check-ups revealed no physical cause. Since childhood she had had dreams of being stabbed and said those dreams were so real that she could feel the knife going into her stomach. She also resisted going to school because she saw no point in it—she said she was going to die by the time she was eighteen years old. How did she know that? She said that she just knew it. Having her place her hand on her stomach and allowing the images to form brought the following story.

(When asked to press the area where there was pain, she saw soldiers, briefly. She then remembered a line from a song: "It's all right till my baby comes home." She remembered the source of pain in her dreams; how she was

Alive Again...Again...and Again

terrified as a child because it hurt. She then described the following event. More details became available as she continued to think back over the event.)

It took a long time to die. I think it hurt. Somebody was there, another soldier. Somebody else. He tried to help with the pain. He didn't give a drug; just sat me up. I think it helped a little. I think he was from the other side. I think he was the one who stabbed me. He was young, too. Just about as young as I. He felt badly. He was crying. I was hurt. I realized he felt bad for what he did. I think I had sympathy for him. I don't think I wanted to kill anyone. I think he was there the whole time. When I finally died, he cried. I think he just covered me.

He has dark eyes, really dark eyes.

(Can you forgive him?) I can forgive him. I think he got killed after I died.

(Why the pain?) **It seemed painful to care. It hurts my stomach to care.** *I think he died the same day—when he had just left me.*

(Were you angry with him?) No, I was not angry with him. I was sorry for him. He might not have died if he had not stayed with me. I think I know him; not then, I think I know him now. I think it might be John. It just feels like it. I think I met him in March. That's when my stomach had the worst trouble.

(Was the pain great?) Yeh, it hurt, but it wasn't great, great pain. I knew I was dying and that's why it didn't hurt so bad. **After I died, I was confused. I didn't know**

where to go. He died kind of near me while he was running away. I think he got shot. He died quickly. He was shot in the back or the chest.

While I was dying, I thought of my girlfriend. She was blond. Was she blond? Her name was something like Sherene. Leaving her behind was the most upsetting. I think I told the guy that I'm supposed to get married. I think he got sadder and cried more.

(What did you look like then?) I had brown hair. I was kind of good looking. Girls liked me. My girlfriend had real light blond hair and wore it in a pony tail a lot—in the back. I think I lived on a farm or, like a place with a lot of grass. It was a happy place.

(Describe the one who stabbed you.) He had real dark hair, dark skin and dark eyes. He was like Italian or Spanish. I think Italian.

(Where were you?) I didn't pay attention to where I was. Near where I died was a hill with lots of trees and leaves on the ground. There were no leaves on the trees. That's where he died, running for the hill. It was cold, but I didn't notice. It was kind of peaceful. He had his arms around me. He was on his knees with his legs apart and his arms around me. He didn't run for the hill till I had actually died. He had a green or brown blanket over me. His blanket. I think the bottom half of my legs were sticking out.

Before the regression she had said, **"Love creates fear. I don't know how to love. Love is just when you care—care for someone else's feelings."** Do you see how the experience as the soldier would create confusing tapes around issues of love? When she was about to feel love, the pain would come to remind her of how painful love is. After all, he loved his girlfriend and that was taken away and the Italian soldier cared for him and look what happened to him. The subconscious mind could record these events and remind her, if she started to feel love, of the pain that might follow. The stomach pain could be the reminder. In the regression, she died at age eighteen just as she had feared in her present life.

Confirmation of the existence of the person in the previous regression came months later in a regression of a good friend of the client in her present life as a beautiful young woman. (That sentence is confusing but I am not sure how to make it any clearer.) Her good friend was regressed and in one of her lifetimes revealed that she was the fiancée of a soldier, Jeffrey Scott, who was from New York and who had died in World War II. She also said Jeff's mother had died and that he had a relative still living in Oregon whose name was John Scott. The friend, in her altered state of consciousness, told us she committed suicide after hearing of the death of Jeff. At the time of her (the friend's) regression, she was dating a Scott and our other young client (the soldier) was dating a Jeff. When these two people met in the present life there was an immediate bond. They were instant best friends and looked out for each other. Both were experiencing difficulties adjusting to their present lives. The one who was Jeff seemed to have come into this life with a lot of anger. Interesting coincidences, don't you think?

Regressions are believed by some to be stories or anecdotes from past lives, or the past of the present life, and that they help us to see the rich variety of experiences available to those who experience themselves as physical beings in a physical world. One can develop compassion for the self and for others by observing the struggles and successes seen in these stories. In the following chapters you will see other themes common in peoples lives today and how information affecting those themes is available at some level of consciousness. You will be shown additional ways to access that information. Perhaps some of the themes or issues presented in this book are similar to your own. **Acquiring understanding by reading of another's struggles—no matter when they occurred—can help you heal your own issues. So, as a peek into a soul's history, a regression is a tool for learning, understanding, healing and enlightenment.**

Chapter II

School Earth?

*S*hakespeare, in the play *As You Like It,* said, "All the world's a stage, and all the men and women merely players. They have their exits and their entrances; and **one man in his time plays many parts."** In a sense, with that one passage, Shakespeare summed up the essence of reincarnation. **A simplistic view of reincarnation is that it is a philosophy that supports the notion that a soul is on a journey to acquire understanding and wisdom by experiencing many lifetimes in this, our physical world on this beautiful planet earth.** Of course, there are many other kinds of experiences available to souls in different dimensions and different other-worldly manifestations. However, those are beyond the scope of this book. We are now primarily interested in those experiences related to and unique to coming into a physical three-dimensional reality—our stage—and residing in a three-dimensional physical body— the actor. Over the course of many lifetimes, the actor plays many parts. **Sometimes we call the theater in which we play these many roles, "School Earth."**

Alive Again...Again...and Again

A very intelligent businesswoman was curious why she was so attracted to crystals and why exercising in water was so important to her. Her daily routine included swimming for about an hour, early in the morning before she began her work. We did a regression to find the source of the attractions and a surprising story unfolded. This is a very well balanced, "feet on the ground," person. Her story started me wondering about some things and also to look at this beautiful earth and our experiences here with greater appreciation. What do you think?

(Are you inside or outside?) I'm inside. It's almost like a cave but it's very light. It's like we're surrounded by crystals. The walls are translucent. This is a different place. It feels wonderful. I don't get a sense of any body (referring to her own body). Everything has a kind of an aquamarine color. I think we came here to get energy or to get energized. It feels great. There's others with me. It's more that I sense them. I don't see them in the physical sense.

(Go to a significant event.) There's a meeting of elders. There's no physical bodies, though. There's a sensation of light. It's a general council. I'm one. We appear to be leaders. The room seems transparent. There is a sense of boundaries, but more a sense of light and color rather than structure. We're leaders of beings like ourselves. It's either on earth before we knew it or . . . it's earth but not as we know it.

(Will you please explore the earth?) There is lots of water. I don't see humans. There are dolphins. In fact, we play with the dolphins. We get into the water with them. To see us in the water is like seeing a clear jelly. A reflection. We just float around. The dolphins can kind of bat us around. It's fun. We communicate with them.

We don't seem to be concerned with eating and sleeping. We're concerned with the planet and governing ourselves. We're on earth in preparation, perhaps, for humans. I think we did come from another planet but don't sense it occurred recently.

(Do you reproduce?) Yes. It's a "breaking off." There's no sense of male or female. It's a nice existence. Get a sense we get old but not age—no physical deterioration. We get wiser. When we choose to leave, we do. The crystals regenerate us, feed us. We don't eat. We don't sleep. We do rest—an absence of thought. We play and we think.

We are, it seems, trying to help organize animal life with the help of the dolphins. The planet is very chaotic and we're trying to organize it so humans can live there. We're trying to understand what the animals will need and the plants will need and what humans will need. I feel our home and meeting places are connected with the water. I don't get a feeling there's much land around—don't get a feeling we're airborne.

*There's an intense sun. An **intense** sun. It's huge. I get a feeling it's there to dry up some of the water. It's vaporizing. It is drying up some of the water. This takes place over a long period of time, but land starts to be exposed. The sun gets smaller—it could be a function of us moving farther away. For this we had help from energies off the earth. Earth was sent out into a different orbit—one that would allow new lifeforms to live on it. That sun energized us. It had no harmful effects; I have no sense of temperature.*

(Later.) I've made the decision to leave earth. I have a sense of being in space—no longer have the jelly part of our

Alive Again...Again...and Again

body. Back to light. It's as though my job was completed. I served a function for earth. I don't get a sense of travel so much as a time or dimension.

(What awaits you there?) Rest. I also get a sense of continued pursuit of intellectual things, but of things I want to learn about myself.

I get a feeling humans may have been an amalgamation of various life forms and they were brought there as adults. They were guided by us initially. We watched them. We weren't sure how they'd do. They had to learn to take care of themselves. Loved them. It was so long in coming. Much went into this. We learned as they learned. Inhabitants of earth didn't have the knowledge when born. They had to learn.

There's great satisfaction and no sense of us feeling superior. They were learning things we would never experience. We were not able to experience what they did. Our group was to prepare the planet. We ourselves were not able to exist in the environment we created. We could exist only in water. Other energies were able to manifest there and be successful.

At this point I did have the option to come into the physical. Much has passed since then. **Many who were involved in the development of the planet developed a love for it, and the humans, and it became important to experience it in some fashion. It is a unique existence.**

Alive Again...Again...and Again

UNIQUE EXPERIENCE

Could it be that this planet was developed as a place for souls to experience existence in a way not possible in any other place or dimension? Ludicrous? Perhaps? Yes, there is a uniqueness to the experience of the physical world. Emotions are one of the aspects of the physical world. **Emotions are one of the aspects of the physical experience that are not available in other types of manifestations,** at least not in the way we experience them as physical beings on planet earth. **Maintaining a physical body is another unique aspect of a physical incarnation.** Many of us who revel in the use of the mental and the sensations from spiritual connectedness often neglect the care and maintenance of the physical body. Yet, that is the vehicle through which a soul participates in the rich variety of experiences available from a physical incarnation.

DEFINING SOME TERMS

So, what are we saying? Perhaps a definition of terms would be useful at this time. Already some terms have been used which may not be familiar to you. Keep in mind as these terms are discussed that this work is not intended to be a scholarly discussion or scientific explanation of words or phrases used differently by various communities or systems on our planet. Certainly, the scientific community would not agree with the definitions that follow.

Dimensions refer to the perceived boundaries of an experience. For example, a pencil point on a piece of paper can be perceived by me as having only one boundary, a point. It is not perceived to have width, length, or depth. A box drawn on a piece of paper might be perceived as having two boundaries—width and length, but not depth. A box sitting on a table may be perceived as having three boundaries— width, length and depth. It is often described as three-dimensional. We are said to live in a three-dimensional world. At least, that is the perception of most of us. **Perception refers to how it appears to the person doing the observing.**

Albert Einstein, the physicist who challenged our perceptions of a three-dimensional physical world, suggests that **time is another boundary that helps define an experience.** How does the factor of time affect a perception of an experience? When I was a young girl studying Einstein's Theory of Relativity, I read a little limerick that was written to help with the understanding of relativity, and it has always stayed with me. I don't know the author or whether it is part of other writings about Einstein, but it went something like this:

> *There once was a lady named Bright*
> *Who traveled much faster than light.*
> *She started one day on her relative way*
> *And came back on the previous night.*

Now, does that not boggle the mind?

A world of four dimensions would have as perceived boundaries width, length, depth and time. Suddenly we are talking about a world that most of us cannot even imagine. What would a world be like that had five or six dimensions? What if there are aspects related to electromagnetic fields in which matter—that which appears to have substance— behaves in ways totally unfamiliar to us? What if there are no boundaries, but our shared belief system causes us to think there are?

Alive Again...Again...and Again

So, the experience on earth in the physical seems to have a lot to do with perceiving the world as three-dimensional and learning to function within that environment. At times, some inhabitants have glimpses of "something greater" but for the most part, we move about the planet with a shared perception of its boundaries. This three-dimensional world is also generally referred to as the "physical plane," based on the perception of a physical experience.

"Manifest" is another word that will be used quite often. In the context of this work it will refer to "bringing into awareness." It is a creative process. There are believed to be some highly evolved beings on the planet who can manifest a stone in the palm of their hand, but we are not often referring to such manifestations as that. More often, we'll be referring to how lifestyles, emotional states, thought patterns, and states of mind can "manifest" or become illness or learning situations within one's life experience.

While all that you experience on this physical plane has to do with the "whole" person that you are, we will often take you apart to look at aspects of that whole that may be out of balance, or are not getting enough attention, or are getting too much attention. The divisions that I use will not agree with all philosophical systems, but will be helpful in understanding our future discussions of the parts of the "Self" or the whole. Those parts are the physical, the emotional, the mental and the spiritual.

Other systems may refer to the physical, etheric, astral, mental, and soul. To debate the correctness of any given system would accomplish nothing, for words used to define concepts in any given culture must relate to that culture and the thought patterns of that culture. There are different styles of thinking even within a culture. That's why **teaching a concept one way for all does not necessarily result in learning or understanding for all.** What may be an "ah ha experience" for one may be a "ho hum" experience for another. I'm sharing with you a system that seems to work well for some.

PHYSICAL BODY

By physical, I include that part of you that can be quantified, touched, that has substance. Also, within the concept of the physical self, I include that energy field that is the battery for the physical. That energy field is like a template or pattern for the physical without which, some believe, the physical body would not exist. This battery or energy template is often called the "etheric body." Much healing of the physical body is done by working with the etheric body. It is believed by some to be that part observed in Kerlian photography—special photographic methods that show a kind of glow or field around living and non-living matter.

EMOTIONAL BODY

The emotional body refers to that part of self that feels without touch. It has been said to be the point where spirit meets the physical. Emotions refer to that range of reactions we call anger, sorrow, love, hate, fear, sadness, depression, and many more. Emotions like anger or sorrow can be spontaneous reactions to specific stimuli or they can be more pervasive states of being like depression or fear. **They are a major part of what is unique about the physical experience and what presents some of the greatest opportunities for learning.**

MENTAL BODY

The mental body refers to that part of the self that creates thoughts or patterns of thoughts. A thought pattern might be: "You can't do anything right. You don't deserve any better than you're getting." Another more positive thought pattern might be: "You are part of the divine spirit and love yourself and all others on the planet." It is not limited to the brain. In fact, a controversial theory is that there is a mind which is an accumulation of all that you have experienced—past, present and, possibly, future—and that this mind permeates the entire body and energy fields. It manifests through parts of the brain and the cells of the body. In other words, the brain and body cells may serve as receptors for this "mind." One aspect of "mind" may be like a computer in that it records all that has taken place but gives no qualitative analysis to those events. For instance, it may record an experience in which a person was humiliated by having to speak before the class and forgot everything he was supposed to say. The computer records the physical reactions to the embarrassment such as blushing, sweating, shaky knees, and inability to think clearly. Whenever that person is again in a similar situation, the computer remembers the reactions and replicates or produces them again. Possibly this aspect of mind is what we call the "subconscious mind." Thoughts affect the emotions which affect the physical body.

SPIRITUAL BODY

The spiritual body refers to that pure essence which can be called Spirit, the Christ Self, the God Self, the emanation from God, the High Self, or whatever you want to call it. It refers to that highest aspect of Self, which is beyond the clouding from physical world concerns or emotions or thought patterns. **It is pure unconditional, non-judgmental love. It is that which is your purest essence, that which stays with you as you drop the layers of pain, confusion, and misconceptions that have accumulated around your essence, affecting your perception of who you really are.** It is that part of you that is connected to the Oneness or the "all that there is."

Spiritual Body or Soul?

Is the spiritual body the soul? Some philosophical systems would say "yes" and some would not. For the purposes of this book, I will use the words interchangeably. However, my perception is that the spiritual body consists of both Spirit and soul. **I think of Spirit as universal and shared by all creation and part of that "oneness." I think of soul as an emanation or ray of Spirit which has some aspects of what we call personality and is unique from all other aspects of Spirit.** Soul might be considered the creative aspect of Spirit which is journeying through the various dimensions of the universe contributing to the richness and diversity of Spirit. It is in this sense that we are considered co-creators with God or Spirit or whatever term you would like to use. I like the saying that "we are the hands and feet of God." Therefore, **I will use the term soul to refer to the highest aspect of the Self, which is made up of the pure Spirit or the oneness and the highest attributes acquired while expressing the uniqueness possible as an expression of Spirit.** Think about that for awhile and it should thoroughly confuse you.

WHY YOU WOULD STUDY PAST LIVES

Why study past lives? A belief that we should not remember past lives has to do with the assumption that the pain and guilt that could be brought to consciousness would be overwhelming. However, as we learn more about the philosophy of reincarnation and accept that the life in the physical is a condition we choose in order to learn and grow, we begin to see the benefits of such a study. And how do we learn? Just as in school—**we learn from lessons.** So, if the events which have occurred in our many lifetimes were lessons developed for our ultimate growth, then to be "stuck" in the pain and guilt would be to deny the very reason for the "lessons."

Therefore, **the study of past lives—our own, as well as others—helps us to understand the inner workings of the human consciousness and how it adapts to Spirit working through the physical.** It is a most interesting study. What causes one soul in a physical body to react violently to a stimulus while another reacts passively? What behavior is programmed into these computers of ours over time? How do you change these programs so that your reactions to stimuli come from a God/Spirit connection rather than a physical/emotional connection?

You are an accumulation of all the experiences of your lifetimes. Those experiences have made you who you are. One of the greatest moments for me is when a client who was a victim of abuse or incest can say, "I forgive the person or persons who abused me, and I accept those experiences as helping make me who I am and I love who I am." I know people who had terrible childhoods with no support for who they were as an individual. Those people had to find their self-esteem within themselves because no one else was out there cheering for them. Now they are strong, independent, confident people. They know they can take care of themselves because they have done it. This is not to say that I recommend sexual, physical or verbal abuse to help develop strong people. It is just the making the best of a negative situation.

The following is a regression in which life was easy and there was no struggle and the person's comments about struggle and strength after the death are interesting. This person, in the present life, has absolutely no interest in a life of ease. She wants growth. Maybe this is why.

(Describe the vegetation along the path.) There are trees, tall and narrow trees, and green rolling grassy hills and open fences. The fences are marking property. They're wood. They're almost like half a tree—like a corral fence. They are painted. They're white. There's a black carriage with one horse. I'm in the carriage. I'm female and in my early twenties.

(Do you have a destination?) Yes. It's a big white house set back from the road. There are four columns in front of the house. It's a big house and I live there. We drive to the front and there's a woman waiting there. She must be my mother or an aunt. She's an older woman. We're very happy to see each other. I think I was on a visit and I've come home. I'm too old for school. There's a piano. There's a black woman there, too. The home is large. It's lonely. It's beautiful there with windows and French doors, and light and pale colors.

(Later.) My mother is dying. I'm waiting for her to die. She's there. The room is quiet. There's a young child, about

*eight or nine, a girl, and she's mine. We're there in her bed-
room. She's very still. She'll die soon. I'm very sad, but we
know— we're prepared that she will leave us. I think I still
live there. I don't think there's a father there. My father's
not there. My husband is in the hall waiting. We all live
there. She was very good. She's old and she's ready to die.*

*(Later.) My daughter is being married. She's going to
go away. She's being married and then she's leaving, going
to a far place and I'm sad that she's leaving.*

*(Do you like her intended husband?) Yes. It's hard to
be happy for her and sad to lose her. I feel like I'm losing
her. She has red hair. It feels like the South—very beautiful.
It's South Carolina and she's going to the East Coast, far
distant, North. It's a happy place but I feel I'll be lonesome
without her.*

*(Later.) I'm doing embroidery work—needlepoint. The
house is very quiet. I think I'm alone. Still it's beautiful.
My husband is still there, but not in the house right now.
He's out with the horses. We're older now. He's busy. We
don't see the daughter. It feels like I've adjusted to her being
gone. Time needs to be filled. It's a chore to keep busy.
There's not really enough to do.*

*(Preceding death.) I'm in my mother's bed and I'm
sick. My hair is white. I think it's my time to die. There's
no fear. I'm just waiting. My husband is there sitting and
he's waiting with me. His hair is gray. I feel like I didn't do
enough. It was a very easy life—**no struggle.***

*(What was the lesson?) It was so easy. It was very
nice—very pleasant. Maybe, what I learned is that the*

Alive Again...Again...and Again

struggle is good. When you struggle and get through, it gives you a sense of your own strength. When it is so easy, it's not always the best.

(Move to that higher level of consciousness, to what we call the High Self.)

(Was that life to show struggles are valuable?) Yes, that strength comes through them—because of them. The lessons are more clearly learned in the experiencing. They are blessings, really. **Struggling is a gift.**

(For one's growth?) Yes. It's important to learn to dissect them and find the lesson in them and not to strain so against them. If strain so against them, don't understand the lesson. It's important not to give up even though the struggle is great. If you give up, those easy gentle lives are just a rest. **It is those struggles that make the spirit strong. You understand more who you are. Also, not to fear death. Death shouldn't be feared.**

Have the struggles of life made you stronger, or weaker? Or, have you even thought about it? In my classes I often use the analogy of a golf course and the game of golf. What does golf have to do with life and being strong?

Golf Course Analogy

Consider this. You are a golfer who has been developing and practicing your skills for years. Each of the clubs in your bag represents a tool to be used in specific situations. For example, the driver is a tool used only when teeing off or starting the play at any given hole. A wedge is used when one wants to pop up over the grass and travel a shorter distance to a more specific point. A putter is used when the golfer is within range of the goal—the hole—and the grass is fairly even and short with possibly a gentle slope or two to divert the ball from its intended goal.

This bag of clubs or tools might be likened to coping skills used to maneuver through the golf course of life. A true student of the game of golf will have practiced equally with each club so that his game is balanced. He would be at a relatively similar skill level for each club or tool. Occasionally, you find athletes or muscular people who put all their emphasis on the driver and they get out there and "boom" it down the fairway. Everyone exclaims over how far they have been able to hit the ball. They can "muscle" their way toward the green. However, when they get near the green where shots require finesse, they blow it. They may hit too far back and forth over the green so that they cannot get close to the intended goal. When it is time to putt, which requires much more subtle skills and even the use of the finger tips, they are totally lost. **They never have a decent score because they put their effort into only one part of the game. As in life, one needs to be able to use all the tools in the bag**—not just a few.

Golf courses are all different. Some are very difficult and challenging, rugged, unmerciful. Others are glamorous and seductive, looking beautiful but, perhaps, possessing treacherous traps and bunkers to snag the unwary player. Others may be simple, uncomplicated, with few hazards. Golfers who play them may be able to record excellent scores and tell themselves how great they are.

But what of the truly skilled golfer? Which course would

that person choose to play? Would our golfer choose a course that would test every tool in the bag, or one on which a great score could be achieved with little effort? What course would you choose?

Imagine that you are a soul preparing to come into a physical incarnation again. You have experienced many lifetimes with much diversity. You have learned much. You would like to test your coping skills. You want to see if you have the stuff it takes. You want to play *Pebble Beach*. You want to see whether you can drive along the rocky cliffs with the wind against you and keep your ball in play. Can you avoid falling off course or out of bounds and being swallowed up by the ice plant? Can you handle the large undulating greens that cause the hole to elude your ball even as your goal is in sight?

TESTING YOUR SKILLS

If you really wanted to test your skills, what kind of life might you choose? Let's see. I have been with many clients over the years so I think I could design a Pebble Beach lifetime equivalent. I would begin with parents who came from abusive, alcoholic families who are themselves abusive and addictive. Of course, they would be young and would share the tragedies of their lives with each other and swear that they would never be like Mom and Dad. So, here you come. At first, you are like a doll and they are so loving. However, birth was difficult and you are kind of beat-up and sore and you hurt, so you cry. That gets old fast, and soon the parents are fighting and screaming and you cry more.

About a year or two later, another child comes along.

Because the parents have never learned to manage their lives, a couple of other children come along, even though the parents are overwhelmed already. Whenever Mom gets pregnant, Dad gets angry with her for allowing it to happen and he drinks more.

Oh, did I tell you that you were a girl? Well, you are. Dad drinks beer everyday in front of the TV after work until he falls asleep or passes out. He is getting bloated and repulsive looking. You, on the other hand, are approaching puberty and are blossoming. Dad notices. With his faculties somewhat numbed by the alcohol, he starts to make lewd remarks to you and then slips into your room when everyone else is asleep or out of the house. You are horrified. You constantly have to fight him off. You do not tell anyone because you are sure you are the only person this has happened to and it is so disgusting.

Because your parents are so unorganized, you take on more of the responsibilities with the other children and try to keep everyone happy. You try to be perfect. You get a job at an early age because it is obvious the only way you will ever have any money is if you earn it. Though you are a top student, you have given up any hope of ever going to college because there is no support for that from the family—financial or otherwise.

You date. Everyone drinks. You do a little but you never want to be like your parents. Falling in love, you marry someone exciting, daring and unpredictable who occasionally drinks too much and who has rarely talked with you since the first two dates. You feel needed. You have babies. Your husband puts you down a lot and you feel such pain, such emptiness, you drink to anesthetize yourself. One day you awaken in the hospital and you are ready to play the next hole.

This time you decide to sharpen your skills. You came to play a tough course but you became so involved with the course you forgot to use the tools you brought with you. Sometimes you find yourself humming an old tune about being given a mountain this time, one you can never climb.

What are some of the tools you brought with you which might be useful now?

COPING TOOLS

"Introspection" would help. What does that mean? It means looking back over the holes you have already played—where were the traps, the hazards? What tools did you use and which ones worked? Are there some tools that need sharpening or some that are not even in your bag that need to be? Where did you get out of bounds and swallowed up by things that were not taking you toward your goal? What was your goal? Where did you lose sight of the goal? When did you slip off the cliff and almost end play for this round? Looking back, being introspective, examining your life, you see now where the hazards and traps were. You also know where your strengths lie. **You will play this course and master it.**

"Understanding" is another tool. After surveying the course, you have acquired knowledge and understanding about some of the difficulties you may face. You see that life is often like a game and you see the opportunities for growth that are presented by each hazard or obstacle. Sometimes you have difficulty seeing anything positive about a particular situation because of the pain, but you may see later what you learned. Sometimes it may be years later before the positive aspects of a situation are realized. So, **you look at each stroke or position on the course with an eye toward what it can teach you. The understanding helps you feel compassion for others who may find themselves in the same situation.** You encourage them to stay in the game, also.

"Strength" is another tool. With each difficult experience you get stronger. Success or failure, as we call these attempts, contribute to the ultimate success. In fact, Thomas Edison is said to have commented that failure contributed more toward learning than success because one can learn more from failures. You, therefore, can become stronger from the attempts that failed for now you know what does not work. What great information to have! Strength comes from knowing yourself and what works for you. Strength comes from knowing when to be forceful and when to be gentle or use finesse. **When one is strong, one can afford to be gentle; when one fears that one is not strong, one cannot afford to be gentle.**

After all this introspection, understanding, and strength, you realize that you were playing with defective tools before. You were using defensive tools such as rationalization, denial, projection, depersonalization, blaming, all those tools of defense that temporarily get you out of a situation but never quite get you through it. They seem to break down just as you are trying to reach your goal. You now recognize those tools for what they are and use them with the knowledge that they are only temporary solutions.

OVERACHIEVING SOULS

You have brought your ball into bounds. You are back in play now. **You will play this course.** Sure, you will fall out-of-bounds occasionally, but you will pick up your ball and keep playing. When you finish, the score may not be the greatest, but, by golly, you played a tough course and you survived. I often accuse my clients who have selected really difficult lifetimes of being **"overachieving souls."** Yes, over-achievers, just like the kid in high school who thinks she can take chemistry, physics, Russian, English IV, and Calculus in the same semester—without a study hall. Can you see your-self in heaven getting ready for the next incarnation, feeling really cocky, saying, "Yeh, I can handle that? And while we are at it, let's throw in being gay, and Jewish, and let's be born in the rural South. That should make for an interesting and challenging life. You overachievers are such a problem. Some difficult opportunities must be left for others.

Maybe this little diversion seems silly, but you would be surprised how many times people will square their shoul-ders and comment that they have survived and they are proud of it. Clients will say, "I know I can take care of myself and I can survive just about anything because I've done it." Throw in a little dose of forgiveness for the parents who were **"doing the best they could under the circumstances with the tools they had,"** and you have a person who feels pretty good about himself. Oh, some of you may already have been exposed to our above "forgiveness formula" for parents. Many of us "therapists" use it and it may be overworked. The beauty of it is, if you are a parent and you aren't "per-fect," one of your kids may some day forgive your short-comings and that removes some of the pressure. It is so hard to be perfect these days. Believe me, I know.

Alive Again...Again...and Again

The regression which follows is an example of a typical overachieving soul. Would you agree? Did this soul choose a challenging lifetime into which to incarnate or not?

(Describe the vegetation along the path.) It's rather sparse and quite sandy. Scrub. It's a gated area and it's made out of adobe. It's like a large adobe ring. Walls. There are many people inside sitting on the ground with their flowers. There's not a great deal of shelter, just lean-to types of structures—sticks with cloth. There's a great deal of noise and pain. This is a leper colony! I'm female and about seven or eight. I'm with my family and there are other children. I don't have it (leprosy) yet, so I get to go out. Mostly, I have to run errands for others and to gather water. The people outside run away when I come. They're scared. They don't like to catch the disease. I used to go to school, but no more. They won't allow me. So, I spend a lot of time looking out the gate. I don't have leprosy. I don't understand why I have to be here.

(Later.) I feel like I'm being raped. I'm yelling and screaming. I'm thirteen or fourteen. I'm still inside. It's a guard. He used to be friendly to me when I was younger and let me out. He only lets me out to use me now—not often. I'm ashamed. But, I don't know what else to do. I fight back, but it makes it worse. No one inside helps me out. It's a pretty painful place there. They're all caught up. It provides gossip and entertainment.

I still don't have leprosy. I have to take care of the family. If I get outside, I can steal bread. My family thinks I owe them the favors since I don't have leprosy. There are the parents, a brother, and a sister. One of the parents may die soon. My sister, she's lazy. She doesn't help. I get peace sometimes. *There was a baby born there and they let me play with the baby because I don't have the disease.*

(Later.) I can do as I please inside now because I don't have leprosy and pain. I feel free. Getting out allows me freedom inside. I don't let the fact they have leprosy bother me. Doctors come once in awhile, but people don't get to leave unless a wagon carries them off. It's very cruel. My body's free and my mind. I won't get leprosy.

(Why can't you leave?) Society. There's no one to assert my rights—to let me out right now.

(Later.) I'm just kind of walking around inside, observing. I have more control. The guard is gone and I can have compassion now. I want to help them. There's only my sister now. I'm thirty-two. I could get outside. I come back because I want to now. It's my home. I know these people. I fight with the officials when they come to bring food. I make many trips to the council meetings. An awareness is increasing. We need better facilities here. They're treated like animals and they're not. They only have sores on the body and it's painful. I have to express that. People aren't dying of leprosy—they're dying of disease. It's very unsanitary. There's a fear for people to come visit to see. I keep befriending the guards and they keep changing. I'm getting some support—my not getting the disease has helped. There are others born without the disease. Our strength is growing. There are greater numbers. I take the children and will protect them. Verbal abuse still happens. I can't stop the pain—only teach them how to deal with it. I can't stop there being children born.

(Later.) I'm in a church and I'm meeting with the

Alive Again...Again...and Again

priest. *I'm saying my prayers. The church has been giving limited support. It's the church of the Romans, but they need to do more. And, we disagree. We have children who need out and need education. They allow us to roam free. We need shelter and housing outside the colony. We need to learn trades. We don't have animals or grains. Sometimes we're getting new lepers in to teach trades. The children beg in the streets to get money to buy things. It's not enough. There are more of us. We'll catch the disease if not taken from this place. We need to know there's help— it will change. I can't be the strength for all of these. We have to have help. It's very sad. The priest agrees a little bit.*

(Later.) I'm just sitting inside the wall by the gate. I'm about fifty. Some of them sit around and I tell them stories. I no longer have to be responsible. They come to me for help and direction. The children have taken over and some of them are out now. This has been my home. Some people don't know how to leave now. We have little cubicles. It's not lean-tos anymore. We have grass. We can share a community fire and cook. There is more personal pride, now. The lepers are not so devastated. It's not such a stigmatism. Greatly improved. There are doctors who come and the gates are left open and some of the lepers can come and go, but only to certain parts of the city. Much has changed.

(Preceding death.) I'm sort of walking along a road, but I'm leaving the scene. I don't want to stay there. I feel excruciating pain in my stomach, back, and all over. I'm screaming. I feel like people are beating on me, but they're not. I feel I'm being attacked, but I'm not. It's a disease. It's all over the body inside. It's not on the outside. All the cells and organs inside are affected. I leave the body there. People are watching. I'm not there. It was a painful death.

Alive Again...Again...and Again

I'm walking away from the body. I go back to check in. For them to . . . for them to know the damage done. They're trying to find the doctor. My body was going through contortions. I'm fifty-seven. They don't know what to do. They may try to poison me to help me die. People don't want to watch anymore, but I'm not stopping. They need to know what they've done. One of our leaders will help the doctor. He needs to poison me—he knows it's time.

(Is this done to the lepers to help them die?) Yes. Nobody wanted to watch. There were herbs we could gather. We could do it ourselves and then the doctors helped us. The disease had something to do with nerve endings.

(Were you ever shown any kindness?) Later on, yes.

(Move to the higher level of consciousness we call the High Self.)

(Because we began this regression by asking for a clue to the resentment that was felt for the mother in the present life, I had to ask the following question. Was the mother with you in that lifetime?) Yes. She was the guard.

(Was there trauma to the physical body?) Not at this time. Previously. Reminders.

(Was there trauma to the emotional body?) The skin must be shed. It's loosened and floating free.

(Did the guard love her?) Yes. There was kindness, but an understanding of the guard and his dilemma. He was on the outside and not the inside. He could not show that true regard.

Alive Again...Again...and Again

(Can you release those feelings toward that one?) Yes.

(At the mental level— any thought patterns?) The aches and pains. Like being bruised. Tormented and abused.

(What about acceptance?) The power is in one's own hands—take that and forget the rest. Not to feel shameful or paranoid, but to **allow and recognize the lack of control over outside influences,** to be reckoned with as they arise, not before, and not to carry with.

(At the spiritual level?) You must learn to take solace and have help and continue on. Scars cannot harm.

Do you think this person deserves a rest in the next life? Much understanding and wisdom was achieved in that lifetime. What do you think about the statement: **"Not to feel shameful or paranoid, but to allow and recognize the lack of control over outside influences, to be reckoned with as they arise, not before, and not to carry with?"** So many times when novices begin the study of reincarnation and related philosophies they naively accept the statement touted by many that "there are no accidents." This gets many travelers on the path into a lot of trouble because they tend to accept a literal view of the statement, and are quick to feel shame or guilt when events in their world do not go well. On the other hand, travelers whose world is rather smooth assume they are doing more things correctly. One would have to define "accident." There is chaos in the universe and there are many outcomes to any set of actions. Beginners who have the mistaken belief that they can control the events of the universe are as mistaken as those in our society who think they can harness nature. When events occur that demonstrate that "lack of control," some are quick to believe punishment is being meted out by some omnipotent force or that they are thinking incorrectly, and, therefore, bringing on the tragedy themselves or whatever. **The danger in this thinking is that energy is lost in attributing blame or guilt rather than determining a sensible course of action.** Mother Nature has a way of reminding us of this lack of control with her volcanoes, earthquakes, hurricanes, fires, and other such phenomena. These are all perfectly normal for "her," but not normal for us. Indeed, if we knew all the contributing circumstances, we could say the event was no accident. **In our own lives, if we knew all the contributing circumstances, we then could say that an event was no accident.** However, in our typically reductionist—meaning to reduce a thing or a thought to a narrower sense—way of thinking, we look for quick and simple answers or formulas. For instance, we say that thought patterns are things. And, I believe that to be true. Thought patterns can contribute to circumstances that develop in our lives. However, our thought patterns are not the only influencing factor. **We have gone from a society that assigned no value to the power of thought to one containing many overly zealous and well-intentioned students who believe that thoughts are all powerful.**

HEALING AND THOUGHT PATTERN

This attitude is no more apparent than when healing and self-healing are concerned. **In our discovery that, indeed, the mind does affect healing, we have now decided that we are all powerful and should be able to heal ourselves of all illnesses.** Where is the balance? This attitude creates a guilt and much pain for those who believe this way and are fighting illness and those around them who believe this way and are saying how they must fight their particular illness. How arrogant to say to someone who is ill, "What thought patterns do you have that are causing this illness?" There is no compassion in such a statement. In fact, there is no room for compassion in such thinking. I have also seen this thinking overdone when it comes to prosperity, and have seen people riddled with guilt because they cannot acquire wealth. Of course, prosperity does not necessarily have to do with acquiring wealth.

Thought patterns are one of many factors affecting any situation. They can help. Other therapists who work with regression, and other books on regression, have suggested that once the knowledge of the source of the problem is acquired, a miraculous cure occurs. Occasionally that happens. Most often, however, **that acquired knowledge is just part of the puzzle.** The individual puts the pieces together, determines how those pieces fit into his or her current reality, and "works through" the problem or opportunity until he or she has some kind of understanding. That "understanding" may change in another day, or week, or year, or lifetime. **And, each time a new understanding is reached, it is equally valid because additional subtleties have been discovered.** There are many ways to look at such a process. You might visualize a spiral which, upon completing each cycle, you come back to the same point, but on another level. Or, you might visualize an onion. Each time it is peeled, you can say that you have peeled the onion and you know about the onion. However, peeling another layer reveals a dimension you had not seen in earlier peelings. **So it is with life. There are many subtleties to be experienced. No two experiences are the same for any two people.** Reasons or causes for events are not known. Some are guessed, and we mortals work with our guesses. But we do not know. We know what we think we know and do the best we can with the knowledge we think we have. Fully realized Masters such as Jesus or Buddha can influence more factors than we, but our attempts at seeking positive influence on our circumstances is admirable and worthy of the effort. But, **to assume we have accomplished that kind of control at this stage of our development is arrogant.** Be careful that you do not assume that a person has cancer or breaks a leg because of some erroneous thought pattern. Thought patterns may contribute to the situation, but so may genetics, so may an intent to bring a family closer together as the transition of death occurs, or so may the intent to demonstrate to others that there are environmental factors that need to be changed. **Any person experiencing pain deserves understanding and compassion, for no one knows the source of that pain. Truly, the pain is for that person to manage and we can only be helpers toward that end. Our place is not to judge. We do not know the intent or structure of another soul.**

The individual in the above regression came into a difficult situation and made the most of it. She was not able to achieve prosperity or great wealth and, indeed, those conditions do not seem relevant to her purpose for coming into that lifetime. But, she did acquire compassion and understanding. Now, we'll return to our overachieving soul.

GRIST FOR THE MILL

So, you wanted a tough life and you got it. What do you do now? You could cry a lot. Some people get mad at themselves for being so stupid. One problem I discovered when we would have this discussion in class is that there will always be people who feel guilty because they have had an easy life. They will hear about people who were abused, raped or molested and complain that nothing like that ever happened to them. Remember, problems are in the eyes of the beholder. Being raised wealthy can be a problem—so can being raised poor. It is all "grist for the mill." Maybe you were meant to spend a lifetime "kind of coasting" because the last one was really tough. What a surprise it was for me to realize that some members of my groups were going into depressions because their lives were too easy. So, now, when I initiate the discussion about the "overachieving souls," I am careful to take into consideration the feelings of those who may immediately perceive themselves as "under-achieving souls."

Purpose or Theme

Our sense is that there is an underlying theme or lesson for each person who comes into the physical. **No person's purpose is more or less significant than another's. Each is contributing to the knowledge and experience of the entire lifewave.**

In the regressions you will notice that I usually ask, "What lesson did you come to learn?" or "What did you learn from that lifetime?" Some lessons or themes you will see in the regressions have to do with compassion, love, patience, struggle, responsibility, fear, peace, family, alone-ness and others. Future chapters will discuss in depth these aspects of the human experience, with regressions that are examples of those themes or lessons. The following regres-sion is one in which the lesson was patience.

(What do you see?) I see one or two trees. The house

is wood and painted white. It's light inside. There's fur-niture, a table—a low table, stairs. At dinner there's a table with meat that looks like turkey. Lots of people are around the table. I'm female, about nineteen. It's a fami-ly; I'm the daughter. I see the father, but I don't see a mother; just the father.

(Later.) There's a church and I'm getting married. We're leaving the church in a buggy and I'm happy.

(Where is your mother?) Mother had died.

(Later.) He's going away—to the army. He's just going away. There is a war—the Civil War. I see cannons in the field. They're getting closer; I just see the cannons in the field. The men are dressed in blue—the men with the can-nons.

They're there. I'm hiding in the trees. I can see the house. Other women are hiding in the trees. There's a black lady with me and my seven-month old baby. I'm trying to keep it from crying. I think they're burning it (the house). We go. We have to find some place . We're walking. We have to have some place to live.

We're at a small farmhouse. There's a man and a woman—an older man. They're friends. I think they were waiting for us.

(Later.) We're in a field and the baby is a year and a half. We're just in the field—just walking in the sun. I haven't heard about my husband. I don't know if he is okay. We're still staying at the farmhouse and the baby is good—she has fat cheeks.

Alive Again...Again...and Again

(Later.) It's raining; there's[sic] horses and there's[sic] men on the horses. They're in gray uniforms. They're at the farmhouse. The horses are in a line and they're all on the horses. They're waiting. They're leaving; it's cloudy. I have the baby. They're looking for food. They're moving. There's no food, just potatoes and turnips—no meat. We're not starving.

(Later.) It's sunshiny and I'm waiting. I think he's coming home. It's like the train. He's skinny, but he's happy. He likes her—the baby. He's older and he's different. He's hard. He looks sad.

(Later.) I see the little girl. She's pumping water. She's five. It's a smaller house. He's farming. We stayed where we were. The new house is where the old house was, but it's smaller. I'm going to have more children. He's still sad. All the money is gone. We were wealthy before the War. (Where is your farm?) Carolina. South. Out from Charleston. We go into Charleston—it's the closest big city.

(Later.) I had a baby. The house is bigger now. Everything is growing. We're doing better. This is a boy. My husband's happy. Our daughter's growing.

(Later.) The children are getting bigger. He's four. I'm in the house. My husband is on the horse. He's going some place. I don't like for him to go. He goes sometimes; he goes to the city for business. He goes for days and it's all business.

(Preceding death.) I'm in a chair by the fire and I'm old. My husband has died; he died long before. The children are gone to their homes. I've been ready for a long time.

Alive Again...Again...and Again

(Do you see the body?) I see the body in a box in a church. The children are grown up.

(What was the lesson?) Patience. I learned it.

In the above regression, the lesson was patience. After having lost everything, the couple worked steadily to rebuild their lives and managed to have a pretty good living. They did not just give up.

RESPONSIBILITY

A regression follows which has another lesson that is often seen—**how to handle responsibility.** Please note that the client moves freely into and out of the first person. It is as if she slips into the body and plays the role and then slips out to be the observer. This is not unusual because clients find it as easy to be in the body as to be out of it. Is this phenomenon like what we call the **"observing ego?"** When out of the body and observing the events, the person seems to have available to him or her a broader perspective. When I find clients in situations that are too emotionally charged, I will instruct them to move out of the body and become an unemotional observer. They are instructed to report what they see with no emotion. Sometimes it is not easy for them to escape all of the emotion, but, by pulling out, they seem to be able to depotentiate or diffuse the situation. Some events are too traumatic to stay in the body. This client is a very introspective person by nature, so it would not be unusual for her to move in and out of the body to get different perspectives about what is occurring.

(Where are you?) I'm on a rocky path and there's not a

lot of vegetation. There's a big marble temple. I know I'm in Greece; yes, I'm in Greece. I know I'm one of the priestesses. I have long blonde curly hair pulled back. I'm walking toward the temple. This woman is mature, but not old and definitely a person of authority.

(Later.) She's assisting at an operation. She's just really kind of there. She's standing by watching this. It looks like lancing a boil or that type of thing. She has some kind of relationship with this man who is the doctor. I think this is how she meets him. He's operating on a girl slave. I'm there because I'm responsible for this person.

(Is she one of your slaves?) Yes. Actually, I think she's a temple slave and I'm in charge. This one (meaning herself) wields a lot of power, but she takes her duties seriously.

(Later.) They're in a temple and they're talking (she and the doctor). There's a tremendous attraction. They're fighting against it. I don't think she's allowed a relationship. They are attracted, but not allowed to come together for whatever reason. They become very good friends. He becomes a very famous physician. He stays single and perfects his skills. They stay very close friends.

These two lives are marching parallel with each getting older. Both have tremendous responsibilities. She's changed her dress. She has been dressed in white, but now she's more covered up and has a head covering. I think someone else has taken her place as the head priestess. She still has a lot of power, but not the focal point anymore. These two people have stayed friendly, but with time they don't see each other as much as they used to. I think he travels more as he gets older. He was teaching in a school, but now traveling. They're in love, but chose to honor their responsibilities. I believe it was because she was part of the temple. They were honorable people. **Their word is their bond and they take that seriously.** *Yet, they're close, but have a mental relationship. He loves her very much, but because she has this vow of celibacy, he puts his energy into perfecting his craft.*

(Her death?) I think she was bitten by a snake. It's something to do with a ceremony. She has one in each hand—several in each hand. It's a ceremony she's done often, but this time one bites her. She doesn't die immediately, but does die of a snake bite. I think she was teaching some girls how to do this ceremony. He wasn't around.

(Was it a painful death?) It's almost like she's in a trance. Her spirit just kind of leaves the body. It's almost like it was the way it was supposed to be.

(What was the lesson?) How to handle responsibility.

(Where was the friend?) He was very sad. It was like he lost a part of himself. But he's an old man, also. He's on a boat. This woman had to be very famous, also. It's like everyone knew about her death. She was one of the leading oracles. Very psychic. She became a priestess as a child. She goes to the temple very young—like five or six years old. She grows up to be very beautiful. She stays true to her vows. Very attracted to this man.

(Look at this man. Is he familiar?) Yes, but I can't put a face or a name to him. In this lifetime (the one we have just seen) he is tall, broad shouldered, with dark eyes. He has a very kind face and is even-featured.

Alive Again...Again...and Again

KARMA

No discussion of reincarnation is complete without a discussion of "karma." Difficult to define, karma has often been called the "cause and effect" of actions, the reaping of what is sown, the lessons one has come to learn, etc. Many people think of karma as a "punishment" aspect of reincarnation. Punishment is not a word that belongs in a discussion of reincarnation. There is no other being who sits in judgment of your actions other than yourself. Later we will speak of nonjudgmental acceptance and love. **Situations presented in incarnations are lessons for the growth of the soul. The choices made determine the direction events take.** If one made a choice that led to misery or harm to another, then there would be another opportunity to experience a similar situation with, maybe, a slightly different twist to the plot. People are often astounded at how similar their regression may be to what is occurring in their present life, even though the situations are completely different. However, if some kind of understanding is achieved, the effects of the choice are altered. **The understanding satisfies the karma.**

An example I often use in my classes would be the story of the two Roman soldiers who were ordered to invade a peaceful village and kill the women and children. Both soldiers do it—the action. One does the job with precision and thinks it is good to be killing these barbarians because they are not worthy to live in the Roman Empire, anyway. The other soldier kills as well, but he is touched by the cries of the mothers for their children, the pain in the eyes of his victims. He is sickened by the actions of his government and resigns his commission and retires to a life of solitude, introspection and service to the poor. Maybe that is a little melodramatic, but you get the picture. He understood that his actions and the actions of his government were not contributing to the highest good of all concerned. You will often see the phrase, **"For the highest good of all concerned." For many of us, that is our measuring stick for correct action.** Where was the truth and justice in their actions? He learned from the situation and the other did not.

If the soldier who did not learn from the experience were to come back into a life in order to learn the lesson of compassion, into what kind of life might he come? Would it not be useful for him to experience life as a child in a village invaded by some kind of murderous marauders? Though the actions were the same, the understanding or learning that occurred was totally different, and, therefore, so would be the karma accumulated. **Both intent and motivation are important factors.** When the motivation is sincere and comes from the heart, even the most bungled experiences have value.

When something disagreeable or unpleasant happens to someone, you often hear him or her saying, "Oh, it's just my karma." That statement becomes a synonym for: "With my luck, the world will end just when my ship comes in." Well, try using that phrase—the karma phrase—when something agreeable and pleasant happens. You will be affirming the positive intent of karma. **Karma is the process by which "learning opportunities" are presented to you for your growth and development.**

Two regressions follow which were for the purpose of determining the source of digestive problems. They are good examples of how karma works. This person has had many problems with the stomach and digestive system throughout her life.

(What do you see?) I'm wearing sandals and I see wild violets. The house is kind of a cottage with attached cottages on both sides. There are wooden shutters on the windows and flower boxes under the windows. There are signs on the doors so they must be shops where people live. The roofs are funny—we call them thatched. They are peaked. It's an eating place. There are tables and chairs. There's a bar on the right. No one is there.

(Later.) There are a lot of people and the waitress is real busy. There are noises behind the door to another room. The waitress has on a long white apron and her skirts are long. There are big bowls and she just sits them down on the table and everyone helps themselves. One contains something white like mashed potatoes. There are big mugs of beer. The men have on white blousy-looking shirts, vests, pantaloons and long socks. It's like looking at half a picture. There's nothing on the left. I'm just watching. I have female hands.

(Later.) I'm back on the path. It's a different path. There's a big lake on the right side. I have on heavy shoes and big buckles, and I am dressed like the waitress. I'm not happy. I'm younger than twenty.

(Later.) I see a room and the waitress is holding a baby. There's a big dining room with lots of chairs at one table. She's crying. Some man comes out of a swinging-type door and she clutches the baby and moves back. She's afraid of him. It has something to do with the baby. He's a big man. He wants to be served. He's sitting down. A woman comes out of the door and she gives him a plate and goes back to the kitchen. The baby is crying and the waitress tries to hush the baby. There's a long shelf with pewter mugs, but, otherwise, the room is sparse. It's real plain.

Alive Again...Again...and Again

(Later.) It's a home. I think he's the employer. He's the husband to the little woman who brought him the food. She (the waitress) had the baby out of wedlock. He's very angry with her. She just tries to do her work and take care of the baby. She's not allowed to eat at the table. They're kin, though. She's kin to the little woman—they're sisters.

(Later.) Oh, it's a wooden bridge over hard rushing water and kind of cliffs on either side. It's a little foot-bridge. She's standing on the bridge with the baby. She drops the baby over the bridge. She turns and walks toward the right and now I can't see the right side. There are cliffs, brown earth, and trees. There are real tall snow-capped mountains in the background with clouds on top of them. I can't see anymore.

(Later.) She's back in the kitchen with the little gray-haired woman. The man is coming in the door—this enormous man. (The back of the neck of the client is starting to get hot at this point.) He backhands her across the back of her head and she falls on the floor. It was a full swing of his hand.

(Later.) Now I see her in a big four-poster bed propped up with a lot of pillows. She had on a white lacy cap. The sister is sitting on a chair by the bed. She's dying from the wound. There's a round table with a kerosene lamp, a medicine bottle and a bowl of oatmeal with a spoon in it. She died. The little woman is putting a blanket out over the bed. The medicine bottle had something brown in it like iodine—a liquid. Maybe that is why she had the hat on—to keep the medicine off the pillows.

(Later.) I see bright, bright lights. It's like I'm on a

cloud. The sky is dark blue. I'm alone.

(Purpose?) I get the feeling of sin. The baby was the man's. He had raped her, so when she couldn't handle the baby, she threw it off the bridge. That's why he hit her. His wife knew he was the father. She wanted the baby because she had no children of her own. Didn't have feelings for the baby because it was his. The sister is tiny and pale with gray skin. Meek. She seems too old to be the man's wife, but she is. She doesn't want any trouble.

The client's use of the word sin is consistent with our culture in which we are perceived to be judged and then punished. According to the philosophy of reincarnation, she is not an evil person destined to burn in some kind of hell. She is an unfortunate person who was unable to cope with life as it was and made a regrettable decision. In another lifetime she will be reminded by some means of the lack of respect for life she showed with that decision. When she learns the lesson of the experience, the karma is satisfied. Remember, it is her choice to learn the lesson of the experience. We might say that **she arranges the lesson, not some omniscient being intent upon meting out punishment.**

Because we were still looking for the source of the stomach problems, we asked for another lifetime that would give us insight into the cause of those discomforts.

(What do you see?) I see a lot of people and a cobblestone street. There are buildings on both sides, two or three stories high—connected. There's a courtyard and I see an arch you go through. There's a horse and carriage on the right. I'm in the shadows on the left and I know I'm hungry. I'm going to a well to get some water. It's not very

clean water. It looks funny. I have a pole over my shoulder and pails are hanging off each side. I'm blonde and I have braids. I'm about fifteen. I work there somewhere and I don't get to eat until I bring the water back. I see a horse and carriage coming really fast through the arch. I'm on the ground and the water is spilling and the carriage runs over me. Then everyone's gone. I'm gone, too. It's all empty and no one is there. Quick.

(What happened?) She just didn't walk fast enough. Dawdled. The horses knocked her down and the carriage ran over her. It missed her head, but hit the shoulders to the legs. The bottom of the carriage hits the stomach. The shoulders are hot where the carriage went over the shoulders. She's got on a lot of skirts. She's lying on the stomach now and there's a lot of blood. It's coming from the stomach area.

(Purpose?) Very lonesome. She didn't have parents or brothers or sisters or anything. She lived with an aunt in these stone buildings around a courtyard. It must be built around a major road. The carriage did not stop. There are people crowded around. Someone comes hurrying around from one of the doors on the right. He's a doctor. He leans down and rolls her over. She's dead. Some men pick her up and follow the doctor. That's quick; just take her in and lay her in a wooden box. He says the horse stepped on the stomach. Her shoulders were crushed and her legs were crushed around the ankles. He says it doesn't matter— she's dead. He says that she was already dead before the wheels ran over her.

(How is this affecting the physical body at this time?) I have to pay for it—for dropping the baby. Baby comes

Alive Again...Again...and Again

from the stomach. The girl was pregnant that the carriage ran over. I have to pay the price. All I see is bright red mist, swirling. All I hear is myself saying, God, please love me. I am asked to forgive myself.

(We then worked on the self-forgiveness and then I took her to a joyful moment to balance the trauma of the previous experiences.) I'm a man with a knapsack. Threw rocks into a stream. I'm a hiker. I'm completely happy and peaceful. Real contented with what I do. (Had her feel the joy.)

She could not forgive herself for dropping the baby. It was her choice to want to work at acquiring the understanding from the former lifetime. Her High Self, as the highest manifestation of who she is, would arrange situations that would bring the lesson to her attention. No arbitrary outside force imposed a punishment on her. She learned compassion for a person who might be in an overwhelming situation and act in a way not consistent with her usual behavior. What moves someone to kill? Desperation does strange things. **What if we have all been murderers, rapists, saints, prostitutes, kings, and slaves?**

At "School Earth" we learn what it is like to be in the physical under many different conditions. Why? For what purpose would we expose ourselves to such pain? Why do we continue to have babies even when we have experienced the pain? **Conversations with many people in that higher level of consciousness that we call the High Self indicate the ultimate lesson is love—love of the Self, and love of others and all else on the planet. Unconditional love is actually acceptance of others for who they are, and it is nonjudgmental.** Unconditional love and acceptance of others does not, however, mean that you should be with people

who are toxic to, or not good, for you. You do need to be discriminating. You can wish them well, but not choose to have
them "in your space." Try being nonjudgmental of the self
and others for a day—a very difficult thing to do. These are
tough concepts to learn at "School Earth."

Chapter III

Traumas: Wounds to the Self

*T*raumas are wounds to the self and they can be primarily physical, emotional, mental, or spiritual, or a combination of two or more of these levels. Physical sensations or physical conditions existing in the present life are an interesting area to explore with past lives. These sensations often serve as reminders of something which may have occurred a long, long time ago, but which have relevance in the present life. Also, sensations of pain may be evidence of trauma or memory locked into the cells at the physical level. You will recall that at the end of some regressions I ask if there is trauma at the physical level which is impacting the life today.

You might ask, how can something that happened to another body be impacting the present body? Obviously, I cannot prove to you my theory of the process because I cannot even prove to you that it results from a past life. If it is one of those elaborate creations of the mind, then we could say the mind has created the story to help heal itself. All I know is that a pain is usually lessened or it disappears altogether after a regression in which a source of the pain is found. Sometimes the pain becomes worse for awhile. The worsening usually occurs if we have opened some windows into which the client needs to look.

Memory stored in that mysterious "mind" we talked about earlier is, I believe, the source of the memories. If, indeed, "mind" permeates your entire being and records all that has ever happened to you, then, I believe, also, that certain kinds of memories are stored in recording units specific to the function of the part of you that is most impacted by the traumatic memory. For instance, in the regression about the young woman who felt guilty because she could not save her family, we asked the High Self whether there was a trauma affecting the present life at the physical, emotional, mental or spiritual levels. Usually trauma is not present at the Spiritual level because at that level awareness is such that healing occurs. However, a thought pattern often develops in which one asks, "Why has God deserted me?" or something similar. In that earlier regression, there did not seem to be trauma from that lifetime at the physical level affecting the present life. The primary effects of that lifetime were being felt at the emotional and mental levels. There were feelings of sadness, loss, and guilt and thought patterns which played "tapes" that said she was unworthy.

When one becomes aware of the source of some physical pain, emotional feelings, or thought patterns, one may choose to regain power over those reactions. For instance, becoming aware that a certain thought pattern exists, a person can challenge that tape whenever it starts to play. You can acknowledge that something like that may have happened at a different time—circumstances were different, I was a different person then and that tape is not logical anymore. Now, **it is not necessary to know a past-life source of a tape to change it if you merely observe yourself and note repetitive, illogical tapes, and work on changing them.** Those tapes that were established from the present life are often changed that way. Affirmations are also used to change the tapes.

Past-life knowledge personalizes the information and often adds a dynamic to the information of which the person was possibly not aware. Sometimes the knowledge just makes it a little easier to relate to the tape. It the trauma is stored in cell memory, the body has to let go of the memory. If the trauma is stored at the emotional level, one wants to change one's reactions or emotions around certain events. If information is stored at the mental level, one wants to change the thought patterns or tapes that are recorded. Spiritual trauma usually affects the person's relationship to the oneness, to God, as he or she perceives God. When people feel disconnected, there is pain.

An example follows of a physical sensation, that was occurring in the present to remind the person of an emotional trauma. The person was experiencing headaches and, on one occasion, had experienced a flushing of the skin, as when one is angry. This was a client who has put her life together and is ready to experience joy. Just as she was ready to allow more joy into her life, the headaches began occurring. We asked for a past life where a head injury may have occurred.

(Where are you?) I'm walking down the street. I'm going to the courthouse. I'm greeting everyone. They all know who I am. I'm male. I'm walking to my chambers.

Alive Again...Again...and Again

(Are you a judge?) Yes. I'm wearing a wig—it's heavy at times—and a black robe. I'm walking in. There are other judges along side of me. I am in the center. It's an interesting case. The man on trial is there for murder, the rape and murder of several women. This trial has been going on for days. Brutal. I believe that he will not be convicted for as many as he has killed. I believe there are many who will not be known who were killed by him. There's anger—mine— for what he has done.

(Does he show any remorse?) None. There are two women in the courtroom who have survived his attacks. I am surprised they have come forward. They are both scarred and maimed. They identify him. There is anger and tears. They seem so alone. They will have to live with this. He will not be freed.

(Later.) It is coming to a close. We have come to a judgement. He will be hanged. One life for so many does not make sense. In this case it was not unanimous. There was quite a discussion over this. It was behind closed doors. I knew of this man. There was political involvement. The murderer was a well known person. One (of the judges) didn't want to prosecute him. There was quite a lot of anger on our part. It was a long time before he (the other judge) changed. He had spoken of it in the beginning. I was outraged, not understanding at all. What is he doing in such a position?

There must be something that I do not know about. I do not believe this one. There must be some connection between the two (the defendant and the other judge) that I'm not aware of. I'm about to punch this one. If it weren't for the other, it would be (unanimous).

Alive Again...Again...and Again

(Is the murderer from a wealthy family?) Yes. Quite a lot of money in that family. The women who were killed and the survivors were from the middle class or lower. I wanted the death of this man and it will be. The other (judge) did not. And, it will be.

(You won?) That is correct. Not willingly, I might say.

(Later.) I am with friends and colleagues. It is a joyous occasion. There are many people there. Must be about three hundred men and women. It's quite colorful. I am with some who are quite close and they are talking about the trial. I am not as angry. I'm glad that it is over. I'm having fun. I'm enjoying myself. It's a wedding of a dear friend of mine—his daughter. It is good to have so many friends. I am happy.

(Do you have a wife?) Yes. She is quite beautiful. She has a hold of my arm and we are talking. We are quite a handsome couple. I am proud of her. She is loved by many. I think sometimes that I love her more than she loves me, but that's not true. You should see how they all gather around her. Quite an impressive lady. I must take her arm so that I may share some time with her. It's getting late. I think we shall leave now.

It's quite cold outside. Where is our driver? Our carriage is quite a distance away. I do not understand. We've decided to walk toward it. I would have expected it to be more toward the front. He would be there waiting. We usually leave at this time. There is someone off in the distance. I believe it's our driver. I cannot see him—it is dark. I am helping my wife in. He is walking around the front of the horses. I turn to ask him why he is not in the front and that

Alive Again...Again...and Again

is when he hits me. Now I know. He was not the one who was to be hanged. He was the other judge. It was a large wooden piece.

(Was death immediate?) Yes. There is an anger here.

(From you?) Yes.

(Did your wife see who did it?) Yes. She recognized him. He'll not get away with this. She saw him and he turned and ran. I did not want to leave. I was too happy, too much joy, too much in love. I did not wish to leave. There is nothing I can do.

(Was he at the party?) No. He was not there.

He, too, was involved in the rapes. Because they were lower or middle-class women, they did not come forward because they feared for their lives. Many were killed. In the majority of the cases, they worked together. They were brutal.

(So killing you was not difficult.) No. For some reason, I do not fear for my wife. She's very powerful—very influential. If it were not for her, I would not be who I am.

(Go to the High Self.)

(Is there a fear of joy?) That is part of this one's issue.

(Fear of intimate relationship?) No.
(Is the murderer present in this life?) No.

(The other murderer?) No.

Alive Again...Again...and Again

(The wife?) Not in the present life. As a guide, quite present.

(Physical trauma?) A healing process is occurring. The scars are almost gone. By experiencing and being aware of that lifetime, the healing process occurs.

(For the wife, too?) She is quite a powerful energy. The pain was hers, too. Not wanting to let go. The joy. It can also be present in this lifetime.

(Emotional trauma?) Anger. It was important that that be expressed during the regression. There was a letting go during the regression. Feeling more peace and calm.
(What about the experience of redness or flushing the other day?) Many factors. The anger, but also changes in the body and in the energy field surrounding the body. It was a releasing.

(Mental trauma?) No. This was primarily in the emotional. She will still receive slight pain, but it will be released.

Her flushing and the pain in her head were reminders of what can happen when there is joy and happiness. Also, she was angry and needed to express it.

SUPER RESPONSIBLE

In the following regression, which also has a physical component, our client complained of her shoulders always feeling tight, never relaxed. She described herself as "super-responsible." So, we asked to be shown a lifetime which could help explain the tightness in the shoulders. Her story is another interesting example of how a physical sensation holds the key to a thought pattern that is influencing her life today.

(Describe the vegetation around you.) There are ferns and tiger lilies, lots of them. There's a bridge that goes to an island which is sort of like a secret garden. Everything is lush like early morning. Moisture is everywhere.

(Go to the place where you live.) It looks like cliff dwellings carved out of rock. There's a ladder, they have to lower a ladder. It's all pretty open. There are families that have certain sections. I'm male and about fourteen. I have a brother and a sister and parents. I do a lot. I guess because I'm the oldest. I do a lot of work. I get the feeling there's something wrong with my brother and sister. I do more than my share.

I carry water in bags over the shoulders, over the shoulders and down the back. There are two bags on each shoulder. The protected bags are in front. They would burst, otherwise. I have to do twice as much. Firewood, also.

I rigged up two of them, would have to make half as many journeys up and down the ladder. Otherwise, I would never have the time to play. It had to be done daily. It's cooler in the morning. Other families had two boys. My friends got clever with their tasks. They'd be through much faster than I would.

(Later.) We're inside. It's a large cave. I'm there with a lot of my friends. We're painting on the walls. We had to

go get berries. We found the good stuff by the elders. We played elders and did our stuff in a small cave. We had a game we played with sticks and stones. They had to be uniform in shape. One could be square or different. It had something to do with placing stones. It was a fun game. You had to toss that funny stone with lines on the ground. If you hit a stone, that was yours and could be replaced with a stick. I had so many chances and when I finished, another played. Usually four people played, but you can also play alone.

(Later.) It must be a holiday. They're killing and cooking something. I don't like to see that. I don't like to see it killed in front of me. It doesn't have a chance. We're all there. There's some ritual the men do. The women do the cooking. They prepare things like mush and serve it in bowls—there are large leaves in the bowls.

(Do you dance?) I don't like to dance. It's sissy. I don't mind some of them. I know them, but I don't like to do them.

(Later.) I'm outside. I never made twenty. There's an accident. I fell off the ladder carrying the water. It doesn't seem right, though. We're having a race up the ladders to see who can get up to the top the fastest and I slipped. Nothing below except more clay. It's interesting. I'm falling and I'm thinking, **"Now who's going to carry the water?"**

(How did the body land?) On my back—middle of the back. Something hit my head. I'm all broken up and my head was open. I'm looking down at me and my legs are turned, I'm half on my back turned from the waist. They

Alive Again...Again...and Again

*had to get my parents. Father was out hunting and moth-
er was inside with the others.*

*(Go to that higher level of consciousness we call the
High Self.)*

*(Affecting the shoulders today?) No. The connection is
with the thought pattern—"Who's going to take care of
the family?"*

FREE FLOW OF ENERGY

**Another way these various traumas affect the present
life is that they restrict the free flow of energy in the being.**
Life force, Spirit. Chi, God force, or whatever you choose to
call it, flows into and throughout your body and energy
fields. **Whenever there is a restriction in the flow of this
energy there is an effect or consequence.** It may be at a
physical, emotional, mental or spiritual level or a combination of levels. If it is at a physical level, it can involve an
organ, an organ system, pain or any number of physical
manifestations. Please be an actor for a moment and imagine
yourself feeling angry. Really get into it. Where do you feel it
in the body? Now try feeling intense fear, whatever kind of
fear most relates to you. Where do you feel that in your
body? Is there less free flowing energy?

Trauma causes blockage. An ongoing trauma—continu-
ous exposure to situations which cause fear or pain—causes
blockage. In many cases the blockage is very subtle, but over
several years even a subtle, small blockage or restriction can
affect the part of the body where that is occurring. It is as
though the life force is being choked off from the area of the

body that relates to the trauma. A whole system may be affected such as the respiratory system or the circulatory system. Depression may be caused by a trauma, or several traumas, to the whole body at many levels—physical, emotional, mental and spiritual— and causes a general slowing down of all the systems.

Healing can occur when you identify with someone else who may be experiencing a situation similar to your own. You resonate or vibrate to a similar situation with someone else. Reading a story or, in this case, a regression, can cause you to resonate to the person experiencing the regression in much the same way as if you were with that person and he or she related the story to you. I use the term resonate to mean "vibrates with." This concept is difficult to explain. I shall use the analogy of the tuning fork. A tuning fork that vibrates to the note "C" will resonate with another fork that vibrates to a "C." If we could see the vibrations coming from these two forks, they would be similar.

Human beings vibrate. In fact, we have all kinds of things vibrating in us and around us. It is believed by many that our minds send out vibrations that are received by others who are also sending out and receiving vibrations. You may say something to another person and—to use an old phrase—it "strikes a chord" with them. They listen more intently or they somehow relate to what is being said, but do not know why. They may not know for years, or they may never consciously know why a particular sentence or story struck them. But some memory, deeply hidden and forgotten, is often stirred by the words, events or stories which may be similar to, or have some relation to, that lost memory. At a subconscious level, something may have been accessed and change begun. In the presence of the new information, the

"mind" computer may make some changes in an "old tape."
For instance, do you remember the regression about the girl
who lived in the wrong part of town and wanted to change
her life? Someone reading that story and living in a similar
situation might resonate to that story and be inspired to
change her own life.

This awareness does not always have to occur at the subconscious level. At the conscious level you may be aware of
similarities to your own situation and be inspired to make
changes and take control of your life. You may be aware that
you are resonating to information that you are receiving, and
a combination of the subconscious and the conscious can
work together to make the change. Even physical pains can
be affected by another person's story. Perhaps an awareness
or a remembrance of an event of your own which may have
traumatized a part of your body will assist you in healing
that part of your body. Pay particular attention to any information that causes "goose bumps" to form on your arms or
on the back of your neck. Usually that means, "Pay attention,
you are in the presence of truth." **You are reclaiming power
when you pull information up from the subconscious and
choose what to do with it**.

MAKE CHOICES

Choose what to do with it. **Make choices.** Choose to
change tapes that are no longer useful or relevant. Choose to
live your life with the direction of the conscious mind and
the High Self. Consciously choose how you want to react to
situations. Choosing, choices, making decisions, these are all
elements of "will." **Will is that creative aspect of Spirit, the
part that comes into the physical to learn the results of**

certain choices. In the present life, you see the results of certain choices, if you choose to look.

FEAR

Fear takes away your power. You need to recognize and understand your fears in order to see where you might be abdicating power. **Fears are good examples of programs or tapes from past experiences.** Most of us are familiar with the concept of phobias or fears based on early childhood experiences. An example frequently cited is a person with claustrophobia who had been locked in a small dark closet as a child. Clients experiencing regressions, looking for insight or information from the past that will help explain present fears, often relate stories that are credible explanations for the sources of the fears. Afterwards, they report that the fear is gone or that it is more manageable.

There are fears for about everything you can imagine. Alphabetically, **some of the most common fears I see are fear of abandonment, fear of aloneness, fear of failure, fear of happiness, fear of loss or not having enough, fear of power, fear of rejection, fear of responsibility, fear of sex and fear of success.** We will only be able to include a few examples in this book.

Some fears are minor little irritations that just do not seem rational, but cause some embarrassment to the person. One such fear involved a very "level-headed" client who was fearful of an automobile crash whenever she would ride with her husband. She also felt somewhat panicky if traveling too close to another vehicle, feeling as if she were trapped and had no place to go. These feelings were not a major problem in her life, but were a source of some irritation to the husband who did not appreciate her "back-seat driving," because he considered himself to be a sensible, careful driver. Two regressions performed on two different occasions gave insight about the fears and seemed to bring relief.

(Describe the vegetation along the path.) There's grass and sidewalks. It's a neighborhood. We have a small white house with a red roof. There's a yard and fences—a picket fence. There's some furniture inside, couches and chairs. There are brown couches and pillows. It feels like the forties or the fifties. It's light inside. I think I'm male. I'm wearing brown shoes and I'm eight. There's a table and some other kids—a couple of boys and a girl—and a mom. I don't see a father. I'm sitting on the end. She's serving food. We're all about the same age.

(Later.) It's a dance. I must be in junior high. It's fun. The girls have dresses with big skirts. It looks like it's semi-formal. The guys look like Buddy Holly. I'm noticing one girl in particular watching others dance. She's cute. I'm kind of standing on the side. She's got blonde hair. I feel like I've got a crush on her, but I'm kind of shy.

(Do you ask her to dance?) Yes. She's good. We just dance. I don't know her that well, but we dance pretty well together. Seems like there's a group of kids chatting. She's there. I'm there. She doesn't leave. I don't think she was my date. I think we arrived in a group.

(Later.) It's graduation. There's a discussion of what we're doing after school was over. There's a discussion of Korea. And, we're going into the Army. It seems a lot of them are. I don't get a sense of college or anything. There's

kind of a sadness. They're scared about what's coming. I see myself finally. I have dark hair, lean, wearing white T-shirt and jeans, hair kind of pushed back.

(Later.) Now I'm in uniform. It's green. I have boots on. I feel like I'm walking, marching. I keep looking down at my boots. I'm carrying a lot on my back. We're kind of marching single file on a road. There's a feeling of excitement, nervousness.

(Are you going into battle for the first time?) Yes. I'm scared. (Shows emotion and cries.) One boy talks a little about it. Everyone else's head is down, just marching. There are trucks coming toward us carrying people who are hurt. We're getting closer. We're gathering around one man. He has a walkie talkie. He tells us where to go— where to put our gear. It seems like a camp. There are tents. We can hear the bombing. We're still going to our tents and getting ourselves set up, where we're going to sleep. I'm giving general directions. The guy who said he was scared—we share a tent. I think that guy might be my husband now. I can see his eyes. We're good friends.

(Later.) I'm in a trench. We're throwing grenades. We're shooting. They're hiding in the trees at the edge of the forest. We're shooting at the trees. We're in this hole. We throw grenades and then duck. My friend is there, too. They shoot back. They have straw hats tied under their chins. We're not as frightened as we were before. It doesn't seem real to us, though. It's like it's a game. We're all fine. I do go back to camp.

I'm in the mess hall now. Tent. We're eating stew. My friend is there, too.

Alive Again...Again...and Again

(Later.) I'm coming home. I'm in a car driving down the street. I'm going up to my parents house. My mom grabs me at the door—gives me a hug. I'm still in my uniform. I don't see my dad anywhere. My friend survived, too, but he doesn't live in this town. I think I'm home for good. That's what the discussion is about at the table. We're having lunch. My sister's in high school now.

(Later.) I'm driving in a car along a beach. It's a winding road. It's pretty. Looks like I'm on the ocean. The road is curvy. It's sunny out, warm. I seem to be alone in the car. I seem real relaxed. It's a real pleasure to be driving again.

Oh, man. I'm going off the cliff. I'm falling. And now I get a sense that I'm rising. I'm going toward the Golden Light. A truck came towards me in my lane. He beeped just before I went off. He was in my lane though. I was just reacting to get out of his way. I think I died fast. I have a sensation of hitting the car and rising. It was a red car. Pretty. Buick. Cherry red.

(What was the lesson?) About war. Just how vulnerable. I was kind of new and experienced the war and lived through it, but saw a lot of death. The randomness of it— that random is natural.

(Move to that higher level of consciousness we call the High Self.)

(Was that a recent or parallel life?) Yes. Recent.

(Is it the cause of the fear of an accident now?) Yes.

(Did your friend also die shortly after the war?) Yes.

Alive Again...Again...and Again

After me because I did not experience his death. We were good friends.

(How did he die?) Cancer.

(Is there anything we should do to alleviate the fear of the accident or is it done?) Should be done.

(What is the purpose of these two friends to be back together again?) To explore friendship as male and female and to explore intimacy of friendship in physical and emotional sense.

The purpose for these two souls to be together again was very interesting. Perhaps the fear of the accident was also a reminder at some level that these two had been together before. In the next regression we see the source of fear when the distance between her vehicle and others becomes too small.

(Describe the vegetation along the path.) I see mostly rocks and a dirt path. It's fairly broad with gray stone and sparse vegetation. There's a tent, a gray tent, too. It's a fairly large tent. There's enough room for beds and supplies. There are pots and pans in there. It's more a utility tent.

We've found gold. I have really strong hands. I'm a man. I see a crevice that we crawl through. You have to bend. It looks like a crack in the rocks you can walk through. That's where the gold is. There's no sense of light. It's a crack and we keep going into it. It's dark. We have a lantern with us. It smells weird like kerosene, dirt, etc. There's gold in the walls. We're looking back at the crevice about twelve feet away. We don't want to make the crevice bigger because we don't want anyone to find us. We work hard. It's really hard work. We don't get much. My hands are really cut up.

(Later.) We're sitting around the fire. There's four of us. We seem to be pretty jovial. We may even be drunk. I think we are celebrating our prosperity. We seem to be out in the middle of nowhere. Rocks. Scruffy bushes. We're all older. We're not in our youth. I sense we've done well with the mine.

(Later.) For some reason I get a sense now that the mine has become more commercial. There's more equipment. It's more mechanized. The cavern's gotten bigger. Pulleys move the gold. It's much larger. More people are working with us. It's not just the foursome anymore. We have carts, tracks with little cars on them. The opening is bigger. There's more of a cave at the beginning. The cars go into this hole beyond the open cavern.

(Later.) I'm riding in a cart on the tracks away from the cavern. We're in a tunnel with some other men. We're going down to look at something or inspect something. I don't think I do any mining anymore. I'm very old, actually. I dress like the rest of the miners, but sense I am one of the owners of this mine. There are lanterns hanging on poles. We're going down. There's a system of pulleys for coming back. We go far. It's getting darker and colder. Now we're getting to the end of the shaft. The tunnel narrows here. We're discussing widening this passage. "Is it of value to do so?" We'll be moving forward, but also should it be wider and broader?

I have a feeling that the carts crush us. I'm feeling

pinned against the wall and that a train of carts came down. It happened very quickly. It was like they were being pulled and something broke. They were loaded. We had taken an empty one down and the rest were full. When they were pulling them up, something broke and they came back on us. The passage is narrow. We couldn't get out of the way. There was panic. We couldn't go anywhere. I have a feeling I was removed from my body before they hit. I see the body just pinned against this wall. It wasn't very gruesome. We just got crushed.

(Let's do some exploring.) Wasn't married. California. Last name was Hawkins. Southern. It's hot, rugged. Rocks. Death Valley or that area.

(Lesson.) Prosperity. Also, the spreading of that prosperity to others. It was a very equitable situation for all. Also, a lesson in the value of hard work. Had great joy from my work. Felt good about what we were doing—like I knew my business.

(Move to that higher level of consciousness, to what we call the High Self.)

(Physical trauma?) The big joints. Bones. Those that would have had the greatest impact.

(How can we help heal those?) Visualize carts magically stopping before impact or bouncing off them.

(Emotional trauma?) A snap of rope. Panic. Fear. What was that? Only seconds. No resistance.

(Mental trauma?) The amount of space surrounding.

Alive Again...Again...and Again

A conscious thought not to be in a place where mistakes made by others could be a factor. For example: anxiety when space reduced between vehicle in front and her own.

(Spiritual level?) None. I see that drawing the connection between this experience and dying in an accident with husband will be beneficial—not the husband, but the circumstances.

FEAR OF REJECTION

Fear of rejection is one with which many people struggle. **It is the fear for which we often give up ourselves thinking that will assure acceptance.** A regression that follows is one that occurred during a more primitive time, but which is still applicable in today's world.

(Describe what you see.) There is some greenish wheat type of things that are calf-high. I'm not wearing shoes and I'm male, fourteen years old. Dwelling is made out of cloth and sticks and hides. It's like a lean-to, it's open. Oh, it's kind of dark. We eat with our hands out of these bowls. It's like a grain. Two others are present—one is younger and one is older. One is a sister. One parent is there—my mother.

(Later.) We have our clubs and we are on a hunt. I'm going to kill an animal. I think it's my first hunt and we're going to sleep out. I'm a little nervous. I've never been before. Some are young men older than me, but mostly they are fathers. We're tracking one. It has brownish, longish hair and horns. We have stones and we're going to beat the animal with clubs. It'll be hard. This one will be hard. He

got up and charged, but we need the meat. Had to run because he chased me. He butted me. He hit me with his horn, but I'm alright. I'm hurt some. Looks like they're getting him down. I'm going to beat on him anyway, even if I am hurt. I don't like it. It's ugly. But, I do like to eat. I'm feeling weak. They make me drink this animal's blood saying it would heal me. It tastes bad. I don't want to be here. I passed out. They'll have to carry me home. I lost blood from the injury.

We make it home. They carried the animal and cooked him. I don't understand why we can't just eat grains.

(How's the gore injury?) Well, he must have hit a lung because I'm having trouble breathing. I feel it under the arm inside the body. They're making fun of me—the hunters. I wanted to do well the first time. I don't like it. I don't like hunting. Father took me back to the house and left me and went off with the other men. He's a good hunter. He's not home often. He says I'll heal. He has lots of stories. They thought I was being a coward. But, I don't like this stuff. Obviously, if my father was a good hunter, I should be, too. But, I'm not. He's too harsh—he's not gentle. I understand we have to eat, but we could eat other things.

Mother is consoling. She bastes me and we're going to wrap it up, but it will take a little while to heal. The hunters just want to throw water at me to clean me up. My mother will give me personal attention and then we'll have to do it on our own. We're going to cure the meat—we'll need it for awhile. It takes a long time to cook. They throw sand at me and call me names. They don't think it's serious. I just want to deal with my injury. I'm having trouble breathing—that's where I think he got me. Children, too,

Alive Again...Again...and Again

they hear stories—they don't know. It's a time for celebration when we bring meat home.

(Later.) I'm sitting in my tent and someone has come to visit, someone from my parent's village. I no longer live there. It was too difficult there. I healed, but I am limited.

(Breathing?) A little bit. I moved to a village where they don't do hunting as much. They are bringing me news. Someone in my family is gone. I have the trophy horns hanging on my wall. They're the ones the children chased me with before I got them. They're welcome to look at them. I don't like them. I told them to take those horns with them, back to the village. Give them to my sister for her children. I'm sure he (the father) told the grandchildren stories—now they'll get to see them.

(Later.) They're both gone now. I think my father just died. It makes me angry that they come to tell me. It doesn't matter. I don't even know the person who came. He's got a haughty attitude like he just wants to see the person he's heard the stories about. My father's dying wasn't that important to him. I shove the horns at him and tell him to take them and go. He's not welcome. He seems to be mocking me and it's in my home. It was quietly sitting in front of my fire before he came. I chase him and throw sticks at him and tell him to leave me alone. He yells all the way down the hill. They think I'm crazy to be alone. Some wise men come by and they're nice. This was not a nice meeting.

There's an empty spot where the horns used to be. I kind of built my place in a rock.

(Preceding death.) I'm walking around outside—close

*to home. I'm gathering wood. Well . . . I forgot to bring my
sling shot and there's an animal out there. It's that time of
year when they come down. I drop the wood and run back
to my place. This animal is mauling me. It was a cat—like
a bobcat. I tried to struggle, he cut my back first. He turned
me around with my arm. Normally the birds warn me, but
I didn't hear them today. He carried me off.*

(Did you experience much pain?) Some. Yes.

*(Physical trauma?) Maybe where he pounced on me,
just over the shoulders. He knocked me down and I tried to
turn over, but he chewed at that. He dismembered me—
chewed my arm off.*

(Lesson?) Not to fight. Not to struggle.

*(Move to a higher level of consciousness, to what we
call the High Self.)*

*(Is the teasing and taunting the source of the anger and
frustration?) Yes, but with anyone.*

*(Pain attached to that teasing?) Yes. (Showed much
emotion. We worked on releasing the pain.)*

The kind of feelings that our young hunter felt around
rejection are still felt by many today. Circumstances may be
different, but the idea is the same. When someone is different
from the majority, it is often very painful. For someone who
was sensitive, there was not much room in a society that
required brute strength to survive. Sometimes we have to
wonder if it is all that much better today.

Alive Again...Again...and Again

RELATIONSHIPS

Relationships are another area where people need to reclaim their power. One of the sorriest statements for me to hear from a client is, "you can't help falling in love, it just happens." **Those are scary words when they come from someone who has a history of selecting partners who are abusive and who is about to embark on a new relationship with only her libido to guide her.** You have choices. You can choose to fall in love or not to fall in love. With the attitude that relationships "just happen," marriage has little chance of survival. **There will always be many people to whom you are attracted, but you always have choices as to whether it is appropriate to act upon those impulses.** Have you made a commitment to someone—do you intend to honor that? Does the other person believe you are honoring the relationship?

Two regressions follow that were done at the same session. A very successful business woman had a friend who was dear to her. She was interested in understanding the attraction to him. It seems that these two had been together before and had honored commitments and choices that had been made in those previous lives. Though they were not together in the physical sense, there was a deep love between them. They had choices, they made them and they lived with them.

> *(What do you see?) I'm barefooted. It's just green, with tall grass and flowers. I see a big porch. The stairs are tall for me. I'm eight years old and I'm a girl. It's a big hall. No one is there. They're somewhere in the house. I see a man at the head of the table with a narrow jacket. I feel very small in a very big chair. Just me. Mother's chair is empty. There is a lady who cooks. Father clears his throat a lot. He*

asks why I lost my shoes. I lost them while I was playing. He'll hug me when I'm real sad. Mother died when she was having a baby. My father was close to me. He gets very busy running his business. He has a warehouse in town. Newport, Virginia. 1782. Mary Ann Ballinger. His eyes are very blue. He's sad, but he stays very busy.

(Later.) We're having a party. A lot of people are going to come. A lot of people are doing things getting ready. I'm seventeen. I'm a little excited. I think my father wants me to meet people, the right people.

(Is there anyone special you want to see?) Yes, I have a young man I'm very fond of. His name is Jeremy. He works on horseback most of the time. He's an orphan and has taken on a lot of responsibility. Father wants me to meet people of my own station.

(Later.) I'm walking in the woods. Jeremy rode by. We sat and talked by the stream. He works with horses. He has very blue eyes and is big and strong. He seems to be very comfortable. He can go bareback and not worry.

(Later.) Guests are coming. Carriages are waiting in line. Father is talking to people as they come in. I have a beautiful dress. They spent hours on my hair. I don't like standing in line waiting till all get in. There are a lot of nice people coming. I slip away to get a drink of water. Now it's time to dance. We do the waltz and minuet. The dance teacher has come to the house. I'm schooled at home most of the time. There are not schools for young ladies. I did some traveling. I like the dancing, but I would rather talk to Jeremy. People are leaving and I can take my shoes off again. My father says will I ever learn to keep my shoes on.

Alive Again...Again...and Again

(Later.) I am married. I moved away from home. My husband's a banker. It's not Jeremy. He's very kind to me. We have two children and a beautiful home. Father died after I married. My husband took over father's business. We have warehouses and horses. We took the children on a picnic and there he (Jeremy) was. It felt sad to say goodbye. He hasn't married. He's afraid he doesn't fit in. He never told me he loved me. He didn't think he would fit in.

My husband's name is Henry. He's tall and thin. He's much like my father. He's very interested in the business and making it grow. The children and I go on picnics alone—take off our shoes and wade in the water and have a good time.

I have a boy and a girl. I'm close to them. The boy will be going to school away from home very soon. I'll miss him. Everyone sends the boys away. I have to prepare him to go. Girls don't go away from home so much. She can make that decision. Samuel must go to proper schools. My husband likes the military institute. Sarah, she could go to Baldwin. Now she likes to play with her dolls.

(Later.) I see a lot of uniforms. My son, Samuel, is in a uniform. He's a big boy, almost a man. He's at a military institute. He's graduating. My husband is very pleased. He's very much involved in the military. It's 1800. There's always wars and that's why I don't like the military institute. Henry wants Samuel to come back to handle the businesses. Sarah came also and she is beautiful. She sings like an angel and all the boys like her. She's probably going to get married. She does all the proper things. She learned well.

(Later.) Henry and I see very little of each other except at proper functions. I did get involved out at the old house. I had to travel. I ran into Jeremy in New York. We talked and had dinner. He married a very young girl. It didn't last. We enjoyed each other very much. We stayed an extra week and saw each other every day. We never discussed love. I told him when we were younger that I loved him. He's a very gentle, loving and kind soul. He mothers people. I think he's always done that.

(Later.) Henry's been dead for a lot of years. Before he died, he had an injury. He fell off a wagon and injured his back. He couldn't walk. He had to stay home and I had to take care of him. I took care of the business. My husband was amazed. Samuel was not strong enough. My husband doesn't know how much I do. I used to read the books. I read most of the books and ledgers of the father when redoing the house. I'd rather do that than stay home. I took care of him, but others cooked and cleaned. I took care of him until his heart just got bad and he died.

(Later.) Samuel finally learned to take over the business. Jeremy's son, a gallant young man, came into the business. Jeremy never married Samuel's mother. I see him occasionally. He's gone his way and I've gone mine. We've never been able to accept our relationship.

(Preceding death.) I'm in bed. I'm very old. All my children and grandchildren are there. They're worried about me being in bed so long. I fell and broke my hip, but I got better and fell again. They were all upset because I was by myself in the carriage. Sarah has five children—all lovely. Samuel married and he has three children and a beautiful wife. He reluctantly works in the business.

Alive Again...Again...and Again

Jeremy's son, Gabriel, is still helping.

(Following death.) I see a cemetery and a lot of people there. There's a man sitting in a carriage by himself. He's crying. He didn't go over. I comfort him.

(Lesson.) You can do anything you decide you want to do. You can love in different ways. There are different kinds of love.

We then asked for this client to go back to an even earlier lifetime that would explain why the relationship with Jeremy was not realized or allowed to manifest. You will see that in both of these lives there is a great love between these two souls, but choices were made—commitments were made and honored.

(What is occurring?) We're slaves. We're working. It's hot. There's a lot of sand. I have to work and cook and he (previously Jeremy) cuts stone. He's very strong. He lifts, cuts, and chisels. He's good at it. He does designs on the stones. He makes temples, I think. I cook in the kitchen, but I like to dance. They chose me to dance instead of cook. I get to wear beautiful clothes and dance at the parties. Isaiah (the stonecutter) doesn't like me to do that because he says we will be parted. He says that if I go and dance they will take me away. The more I dance the more things they let me do. I can take baths, etc.

(Later.) I teach little children to dance. I make up dances. My hair's very long. Isaiah doesn't like all the attention. He says bad things would happen to me. I keep getting better and better and go to more of the parties. A man came to the house and talked to the master and five of

us went to his house. Isaiah said it would happen and we would never see each other again and it was my fault. I cried. But, I don't like to cook and clean. I get better and better and get nice clothes. Isaiah would come over and sneak into the garden and he said one day he would be caught. I don't know what to do. I can't leave and be a slave. My mother had died in that kitchen.

(Later.) I'm afraid he's going to get caught. I'm going to tell him not to come again. They'll do awful things to him. Dancers can't get married because they can't have lovers or children because they must keep their bodies beautiful. Some girls become lovers of the master. Then they don't dance anymore. My master isn't like that. He really loves to see me dance. He's nice to me. He has a family and is good to them. Sometimes men come and say they want to be my lover, but my master won't allow them. Isaiah doesn't believe that. I'll tell him I have a lover so he won't come anymore. It's very hard to do.

(Later.) I see Isaiah sometimes in the city. He's become a very fine stonecutter. He doesn't have to lift the heavy stone. He cursed me when I said I had a lover and didn't come anymore.

(Later.) I'm sold from my master to a palace. I'm still a slave, but I have a beautiful place to live. Sometimes I'm disgusted with some of the men who come. Sometimes it's hard, but if I wish to keep dancing, I cannot have children. **If you don't want to kill yourself, you do what you like to do best and I love to dance.** *When I see him I lower my head because I have deep feelings for him and I don't want him to know. There's a very handsome guard who tries to talk to me all the time and I like him. He said*

Alive Again...Again...and Again

*he would speak to the master about having me as his
woman. I said I would rather dance. I plan to continue and
be the one who trains others.*

*(Later.) I'm walking down the corridor telling all the
girls to get ready for practice. We're preparing for a big
party. I have thirty-five dancers who perform regularly and
younger girls in training. I'm now very much a businesswoman. The master takes them to different parts of the city.
I'm still in good shape. I make up the dances and can still
dance better than most of the girls.*

*Isaiah, the stonecutter, has a family now and three
sons. I walk by the stonecutter and say, "hello," and watch
his sons grow up. He now has a shop and is no longer a
slave. He received recognition. He also does pottery on the
wheel and does very handsome pieces.*

*I enjoy watching the other girls grow. I've trained
most of the girls that are in all the houses. He says he
(master) makes lots of money from me doing that. It's
harder to find good musicians than good dancers. The
name Helenes comes.*

*(Preceding death.) The ground is trembling and rocks
are falling on top of everyone. The earth is shaking. The
whole house is falling in. I'm in my fifties. It's an earth-
quake. The house where I lived is totally destroyed, all
crushed in. Many people have died. There are just so many.
There are not many left. People are moving away from the
city. The stonecutter's not there anymore.*

*(After death.) Isaiah has come to me. He says we
should have found a way. Life is very short. I put my work*

Alive Again...Again...and Again

and salvation ahead of the one I loved. I learned that speaking out and having your love may have been more satisfying, but you can learn to live without it.

(Speaking to the High Self. Will this couple ever get together?) This love is never quite fulfilled, but it's very important and sometimes love can be there just for what it is. It can be frustrating, lonely, and it can be always there. We've been closer this lifetime, but still do not see that it would end together. Both are afraid of total final commitment. When one steps forward, the other steps back.

In the two preceding regressions, the person made a commitment, first to another person, which she honored, and in the second, to a career. She saw the career choice as the only choice for her to avoid the hard life her mother had experienced. She could not have it both ways. The stonecutter was doing what he loved and what he did well. Cooking and cleaning were not what she wanted to do, so she made a choice. These two have met in the present life and find an attraction, but likely will not come together again. Maybe they are both exploring an aspect of love that is even a higher expression than what we normally perceive.

Reincarnation would suggest that you have had many, many lifetimes and in those lifetimes you have had relationships with a number of souls. It is likely that several of those will pass your way at some time in the present lifetime. That does not mean that you should form a relationship with every one of them. **There may be inexplicable attractions or a sense of familiarity, but that does not mean you are to drop other relationships and go off in this new direction.** Attractions are just that—attractions. Mind also has a thinking component for the purpose of evaluating situations. If a relationship is developing, one needs to know if this other person has an addiction, if this person is violent, if this person shares some of the same values, and after much thought and consideration, one might allow oneself to "fall in love."

Abusive Relationships

The following two regressions have to do with a relationship in this young woman's present life that has had some confusing aspects. **There is confusion around love and abuse.** Because the incidents in these regressions are very traumatic, we were only given part of the information in the first regression. Almost two years later, the client returned because she had stayed in the relationship and was still experiencing confusion around her attraction to this man. She was surprised to find herself in the same cottage in that same lifetime which she had previously experienced in regression. However, this time more information was revealed and that gave her insight into the confusion. The first regression follows.

(What do you see?) I see big trees. There's an old house, kind of like a house in the Renaissance. It's dark inside. There's kind of a small fireplace. I see a table and I sat down, but I don't see any food. I think I'm in the house alone. I'm five. There's nobody in the house.

(Earlier.) There's a lady and a man. I think they are my parents. They seem really loving. I think they just kind of walked out of the door, but I was still there. They waved. He picked me up and hugged me and put me down. I think they're going to be back. They're riding off in a buggy. I'm supposed to wait.

Alive Again...Again...and Again

(Where are they going?) I think it's a town affair. A bunch of people. It's a party in the town—dancing and music. I kind of feel lost there. I think I'm still little. I don't think I can find my parents. There's a whole bunch of people drinking and laughing. People are in my face and they're drinking and they're loud. I'm just there by myself. I don't know where my parents are. (She has gone into town for some reason to find her parents.)

I feel myself running back home in the dark. I think there is somebody chasing me. I really think this person is going to hurt me. It's a man. I really think he's going to kill me. I think he has a hatchet. He killed me. Cut me across. I see the body. There's a lot of blood. It's chopped up. He looks old and ugly. He's wearing black. He didn't like me. He hated me. He just left. It seemed like it was kind of a relief to him.

(Where are your parents?) I think I saw them making love. They went to the gathering and got romantic and went off to the side. They're laughing and having fun. He killed me in the house. When I got into the house and turned around, that's when he got me. He looks really ugly, like a really ugly person. Seemed like he really hated me. A lot of violence.

(When do your parents arrive home?) They're getting closer. They're laughing and having fun. They are having a hard time getting out of the buggy. They are both really drunk. I still kind of feel alive on the floor. I'm going to see them walk in. She's crying. He's crying. She kind of reminds me of me—the mother. Don't know about him.

When the client returned two years later, she reported

Alive Again...Again...and Again

having dreams in which she was trapped and she'd find herself screaming, "Wait, wait. You can't leave me." We used that statement to access the next regression. Sometimes I will take what seems like a "key" statement and ask clients to go back to another time when they felt those feelings, or had those thoughts, or to go back to the first time they had those thoughts. These statements ring true or resonate with the therapist and are useful as keys to access information, as in a computer.

(Where are you?) There's grass. Seems like—feels like I'm right back where I started. It's that same one. I'm still that little girl. I feel fine. We're all sitting down eating. There's more people. There's my father, mother, and me. I think there's that guy there.

(Ask him if he's related to you?) He says, "Yes." I think he's an uncle. [In regressions I have found that we have the freedom to ask the participants for information if we do not have it from the person experiencing the regression. In this case we needed the identity of the man so we had her ask him.]

(Later.) I don't think I went anywhere. I'm outside. I'm outside in some green grass. It's just me. I still feel his presence. I think he's somewhere around there.

(Does he live with you?) I think so.

(Does he sometimes take care of you when your parents leave?) Yes. And, I feel something very weird. Violent. Kind of like he's going to hurt me again.

(Move to a time with the uncle.) I think he's taking me

Alive Again...Again...and Again

somewhere—like down in a basement or something. I think he raped me. I think I'm five. There's a window down there. I think he just leaves me there. I feel myself saying, "You can't leave me down here."

(Did he lock you in?) Yes. I'm hysterical. I'm crying and it's dark down there. He leaves and I'm at the window trying to get out. I see things all around me like big things that are going to fall. I'm still trying to get out. There's a hole at the bottom and I'm crawling through. "That takes me outside. It's dark. My parents aren't there. No one's there. It's outside.

(Is the house nearby?) Yes. I'm just crying outside. I think this is where I go back home and I think that's where he runs after me. I don't think he was sorry. He was just enraged. He was yelling something like, "I told you not to get out." He says, "You're bad and you're going to pay for it."

(Move to a time when he sees the body, also.) They're at my funeral and he's standing right above me. My parents are crying. He's not. It's like there are rocks on top of my body. He's hugging my parents. I don't think I'm dead. I think I'm still somewhat alive.

(Everyone thinks you're dead?) Yes. I feel my fingers moving. I'm somewhat crying because I'm still alive. It's cold under here. They're all walking away. I can hear myself crying, "You can't leave me here. I'm still alive. You can't leave me here." They're going to leave me here.

(What happens now?) I try to get out. I can't get out. Every thing is so heavy on me. I'm crying. I'm stuck. I

Alive Again...Again...and Again

can't get out. I die under there.

(Does death take very long?) No. I feel scared. Screaming. No one can hear me. Trapped. I'm still alive down here. You can't leave me here.

(Later.) I see my spirit coming out of the body. It's overlooking the the grave. I still feel sad. I'm still crying.

(Can you go back to the house and see the uncle and the parents?) He's kind of sad. I think he didn't mean to do it. Parents are crying. All three of them are just sitting there.

I can see myself going, "Why did you have to kill me? "You left me down there to die." He looks sad. I think he's crying like he didn't mean to do it. I keep telling him, "Why did you do it?" He says he doesn't know. I'm like wearing this white dress with blood all over it.

(Are you able to forgive him?) I can forgive him. I just feel my soul unrested.

(And what would it take to rest your soul at this time?) For him to say he's sorry—that he didn't mean it. I think I loved him so much and he hurt me.

(Had he been loving to you?) Yes.

(Go to that highest level of consciousness we call the High Self.)

(What can we do to heal that wound?) Forgive him.

(Is she able to at this time?) Yes.

Alive Again...Again...and Again

(What occurred with him?) He was drinking and drunk.

(Did he want to go to the fair with the parents?) No. He was angry and he took it out on me. I think he had a fight with his girlfriend and she left him. I think he killed me, because he raped me and was afraid I'd tell my mother and father.

(When he raped you was the alcohol in charge?) Yes. He was angry. He was a totally different person. He was hitting my head against the floor and telling me to be quiet. I think I had run out to find my mother and father and he was afraid I'd tell them. I ran back into the house and that's when he ran after me. He was angry. I told him I was going to tell my father and mother what he'd done and he said I couldn't do that. He was really violent.

(Did the parents ever find out?) No. He never told the parents.

(Visualize this man and say to him what you'd like to say.) I just want to rest in peace. I forgive you for what you've done. Let me go.

(What does he say?) He says, "I'm sorry." I'm hugging him goodbye.

(Are you able to release him?) Yes. I feel happy.

(At peace?) Uh huh.

(Any other message from the High Self?) To go on living your life and put things behind you.

Alive Again...Again...and Again

My sense is that the other soul, the uncle, was desirous of forgiveness and was needing to be with this one in order to accomplish that. The client said she did feel more peaceful and felt that the attraction to that other soul had changed. It seems that there is much freedom in regressions to obtain more information and to communicate with others. You will note that when we wanted to know the relationship of the murderer to the client, we simply asked him and he answered. I do this often when information is needed that is not readily available. Also, by visualizing the uncle, the client was able to go through the process of forgiving him. This is a very valuable tool because the person needing to be forgiven is rarely available. Yet, the visualization seems to have the same effect as if the person were standing in front of the client. This also works well with deceased parents or others in the present life one might want to forgive or with whom one wants to reconcile. Hopefully, she has a clearer understanding of the relationship and can make clearer choices based on the clarity.

Exercise the "will." You have it for a reason. One might say it is the greatest gift that the divine, or God, or the Oneness can give you. Yet, it is the least used. "Will" here is in contrast to willful, which refers to wanting to do what one wants to do when one wants to do it. That is in definite contrast to "will" as we have presented it here. The "will" to which we refer is reflective, introspective, and connected and open to the highest aspect of an individual, the High Self. After all components are considered, decisions are made as to which relationships are appropriate. **If a relationship is abusive you have to ask yourself what you can learn from that relationship and then extricate yourself as soon possible.**

Chapter IV

Who Are You?

Who are you? What is your essence? **Remembering who you are, being true to yourself, being honest and truthful is not as beneficial to others as it is to you—to your own self-esteem or the regard with which you hold yourself.** Every time you lie or cheat or injure another person, you chip away at that self-esteem until, in some cases, there is little left. One evening I was watching a television newscast. A reporter had done a survey or was reporting on a survey in which people were asked what they would do if their bank's automatic teller gave them $200.00 more than they requested. If I am recalling accurately, I believe about 70% of the people said they would keep the money and not report it to the bank. How sad. How many tormented people do you know who have been so caught up in their own deceptions that they can no longer find peace within themselves? **And, in this busy complicated world, if one cannot find peace within oneself, there are not many other places in which to find it.**

The Need to Receive

This "need to deceive" is one of the greatest tragedies of addictions. When the need of some activity or substance—in order to find peace—is so strong that the person feels forced to lie and do whatever is necessary to satisfy that need, the person feels shame and guilt. **To protect the ego from disintegration, defense mechanisms such as denial, rationalization, projection, blaming, and others must be used.** Unfortunately, these defense mechanisms separate the person even more from who they really are. And, they do not help resolve the situation or solve the problem.

Soul's Purpose

One of the purposes for all souls to come into the physical is to remember who they are? Does that sound silly? If, indeed, everyone is an emanation or spark of this pure Spirit we talked about earlier, then everyone must have a core that is pure and untainted—to use words that are not exactly accurate. So, once we know this, there is a different attitude toward life. **The experiences in a lifetime become—to use my favorite saying—"opportunities for growth, cleverly disguised as problems." Think about how this change of attitude affects perceptions of the world.**

You then become an individual on a quest to learn all you can about what it is like to be in a physical body and a physical world without getting "bogged down" or "caught up" in the drama. By keeping an awareness that the "real" you is perfect and loving and joyful, those activities that take you away from that awareness are merely "lines in a play" that are to be studied and understood. Remember, too, that **you**

are the author of your own play. You are not restricted by the parents you selected or the socio-economic strata into which you were born. **All you need to do is to change the tapes, change the perceptions about yourself to what you desire.** The following regression is about a girl who was born on the "wrong" side of town to a sleazy father and was involved in activities that were questionable. She changed the perception of herself and gave herself permission to leave that life without looking back. The client was looking for insight into issues around trusting and believing in the self.

> *(Go to a lifetime that will add insight into issues of trusting and believing in the self.) I see a path. There are houses. They're like Pinnochio houses. The street is cobblestone. I'm going to my house which is also a store. It has something to do with coins. We're not well-to-do, but we're comfortable. Things are shiny and nice and clean. It's like we sell coins or something. I see a father and he's very nice to me. Maybe . . . he's not. Now I'm getting the feeling he's wanting me to do dishonest things. Now things don't seem so bright and cheery. It's in a bad part of town. He wants me to steal something or do something. Wants me to be a prostitute. That's where I get the coins. I bring back the coins. I don't like my father. I just expect that life.*

> *(Later.) I wander the streets. I have a mission; it's to get money. I'm a beggar. I'm not seeing prostitution. Beggar. He wants me to do it. I see people giving me money for something he's told me. People give me money and I'm taking it back to him. I'm going to doors and telling people what he tells me to tell them. I'm like a puppet for my father. It's dangerous. They're not nice people and it's in a bad part of town.*

(Later.) I'm in my twenties. I'm just a go between. There's no reason for people to talk to me. Other people I pass seem to know what I'm doing and they don't think highly of me. I don't take very good care of myself.

(Is your father like a loan shark?) Yeh. Something like that. I'm female and I don't like what I'm doing. It might be something even more illegal.

(Like blackmail?) Maybe. The attitude of the people is bad. They are mostly men. They seem to know who I am. I stand at the door and they give me coins.

*(Later.) I see a lot more light. I think **I'm realizing that it doesn't have to be like that.** (She's changing the program in her computer.) I seem attracted to the way other people live. I'm upset with the way we live. I see more light in other parts of town. I want nicer clothes, but I know I have to go back. I seem to be staying more and more from this house—on my own. I want nicer things, I want to improve myself, somehow.*

*(Later.) I feel like I've left that house and I'm working in a city. There are more stores and things. I've broken away from my father and I feel pretty good. I feel cleaner. I'm working in some shop and I have nice clean clothes. I don't see my father or miss him. **I let go of that lifestyle.***

*(Later.) I seem to have friends. I'm getting married. I live a very simple life with this person. It was good. I never seem to think about the past. I just enjoy what I'm doing. **I like myself. It was not a good beginning, but it was a good ending.***

Alive Again...Again...and Again

> *(Death.) I think I was fairly old. I had gray hair. I was just lying in a bed with white sheets. I expect to die. My husband's already dead. I don't see any children.*
>
> *(Lesson?) Letting go of the past.*
>
> *(Message from the High Self?) Let go. Move ahead.*

She remembered who she was and that she did not have to stay in the situation in which she found herself. She regained her self-esteem by making choices that supported her growth.

Let us go back to the bank's automatic teller window. A person with the awareness we just described is given $200.00 too much. It just so happens he has a $200.00 car payment due and he could really use the money and so, for a second or two, he is tempted. Then...he remembers why he is here. **He is here to learn and grow in wisdom and to remember who he is and who everyone else is.** To steal that $200.00 from others, and a bank is made up of others, does not contribute to the purpose for being in the physical. Granted, this sounds too easy and certainly more than a little idealistic. Something was learned from the experience—how easy it is to get caught up in the perception of the physical world and lose sight of that purpose.

ADDICTION

What of our addicted person? There is a real mess, you think. Our whole society is addicted if you consider some of the social rituals around alcohol and sex. For a person addicted to either of these or to eating or other activities, it is difficult, first, to realize that one has an addiction because everyone else seems addicted. Unfortunately, it is not until one starts to have problems that the thought crosses his or her mind. Sadly, we see too many people, especially young people, who had a parent or grandparent with a drinking problem, who insist on drinking while affirming they would never become like their relative. Do they think the relative was born with a beer can in his or her hand? Of course, the relative did not present problems right away either. **Addictions build.** Another delusion we see are wine connoisseurs who are really alcoholics. Society accepts this as a much more acceptable form of addiction—it has class.

Therefore, **the first opportunity for learning is the recognition that some substance or activity is controlling or starting to control your life.** How do you know that? Many excellent books are available on addictions and some have self-tests that are useful. A simple question to ask yourself is, "Do I have a relationship with this substance or activity?" Relationship refers to a connection. A relationship with another person can be an addiction. Does it have some connection to you? If your doctor said to you, "I'm sorry, but you must stop eating broccoli because we have determined that it is poison to you." What would be your reaction? Feel that reaction in your system. Does it grab you somewhere? You'll live, right?

Now imagine the same doctor telling you that you may never have wine again, or beer, or pot, or chocolate, or sex outside your marriage, or whatever substance or activity you value. What reaction do you have? Where do you feel it? Is it stronger than the reaction for broccoli? For some, there might be a feeling of panic. Others, who are well-defended, might say, "No problem, I could give it up anytime." One of the most interesting rationalizations for not giving up smoking these days goes something like this:

> *I was going to quit, but now I'm not because of the way smokers are being treated. Now it's a matter of principle and my rights.*

When we speak of activities that are valued, we are not referring to those that are beneficial to the person or to loved ones. For instance, a person may have a passion for fishing and may try to go fishing whenever there is time available. However, the passion becomes addictive when one begins to be driven to go fishing and starts to give up relationships with loved ones and other necessary behaviors such as work. Any activity that would ordinarily be considered beneficial such as exercise or meditation can become an addiction. **These activities often serve the purpose of isolating one from interactions with others and masking the pain.** At some point, a person may cross the line.

Working with our own addictions—thought patterns can be addictions, too—gives us valuable information about ourselves and, therefore, others. Remember, we are all connected. The Twelve Steps of Alcoholics Anonymous, developed by the founders of Alcoholics Anonymous, have proven to be, possibly, the most successful method of managing addictions that we have seen. The process includes recognizing the power the substance or activity has over ones life, recognizing a Higher Power, which could include the concept we call the High Self, and doing self-inventory and self-study. **Know Thyself.** Learn from the situations that have been presented to you. People working the Twelve Steps have a blueprint or a framework in which to learn about themselves and others. **Every time one hears another** person's story and accepts that person for who he or she is, a part of oneself is accepted. Every time a part of oneself is accepted, for whatever it is, then others are accepted, also. Gradually, self-esteem is rebuilt and you become much more aware of how precious is that sense of self—who you are—and how easily it is damaged.

That kind of insight from such an analytical approach to life serves us well. **To be able to "step aside" and look at what is happening without emotion can provide information missed when you are engulfed by the situation and not able to remember who you are.** Please do not assume from this discussion that you are to be constantly analyzing every action and thought. It is also important, at times, to just be. This means allowing spontaneous reactions. If those reactions feel constricted or painful, then we might need to analyze what is happening. Also, if we are finding our lives to be unmanageable, we need to analyze. If you determine that there is addiction, you might need to be hyper-vigilant and analyze often.

Ego

Ego is a concept related to this discussion. For the purpose of our discussion, **we shall refer to ego as that aspect of mind, which is between the sub-conscious and the High Self.** If there were a range or a scale between the subconscious mind and the High Self, and the subconscious were at one and the High Self were at ten, I would place ego somewhere between two and five. That position may not be immediately obvious. However, we only have one word for ego when, in fact, we could use several.

Perhaps the notion of a low-ego, a middle-ego, and a high-ego would help. Let us say the low-ego is just above the subconscious mind. If you will recall, **we used the term subconscious mind to refer to the mechanical gathering of information such as the recording of information or experiences on a tape or in a computer.** There is not an analytical component. "Just the facts." **Low-ego could refer to the ego state that is not much beyond the recorded tapes.** As the tapes play, this ego would do very little analyzing or questioning of the material that comes, and it would defend actions coming from the "automatic tapes." A person functioning at this level of ego would be the opposite of introspective.

Middle-ego might refer to an increase in analytical activity. Some insight or learning has occurred and is occurring. Perhaps the ego has observed that anger and violence, whenever one does not get ones way, is not always the most successful response. The person moves a little beyond the physical self. Perhaps the ego has begun to observe the culture in which it finds itself and deduces that actions of the majority should be the model. What if there are "group tapes," or "shared tapes," or "computer programs" that any given culture accepts at any given time? For example, let us suppose that some "group tapes" that a Western culture in the 20th century might accept are: success is measured by wealth, the clothes make the person, drinking is sophisticated, my country right or wrong, money is the root of all evil, white is better than black, and others, which I am sure you could add. And, if we were to propose that the majority of the people on the planet function at a middle-ego level most of the time, a person functioning at this level would probably attempt to be like "the norm" or normal based on what he perceives to be occurring around him.

CHALLENGING GROUP TAPES

Reincarnation challenges those "group tapes." If experiences are learning opportunities, what difference does it make if you are rich or poor, black or white, Chinese or Russian, or whatever? They are all just different kinds of experiences. For example, in the same session, I often have people go to lifetimes in which they were very poor or even very primitive, and then go to a lifetime in which they are fabulously wealthy. In fact, I would say that happens more often than not. The following two regressions are such an example. These were done at a single session with one client. Yet, the lives are totally different.

(What is the vegetation like along the path?) I see moss—ferns and moss. There are white flowers and a stream with trees around it. There's a wooden house and it has columns in front. There's a porch. It's in the shade. It's kind of darkish, but very pretty. I'm male and thirty-six. There's furniture inside and it's light. There's a table with a bowl and something like oatmeal. I think a kid prepared it.

(Yours?) Yes. It's a long table and I'm sitting at one end and the kid is sitting at the other.

(Earlier.) It's a marriage at a chapel. There are a lot of people. It's outside in front of the chapel. Lots of people are sitting on wooden folding chairs. They're throwing rice. I'm getting married. We're very young, maybe fourteen. I can't see who I'm marrying. We're going to a body of water—a lake or sea. It's a trip.

(Later.) It's the birth of a baby in the house I described

Alive Again...Again...and Again

before. I think my wife died in childbirth. Had a bad feeling. At first I didn't know whether it was a birth or funeral. It's a boy.

(Later.) I'm in the woods and there are some animals. I see some people in a distance. Maybe it's a hunt. Maybe it's something bad happening to me. I don't seem to be happy about the hunt. I'm watching. I'm black. Maybe the hunt is something I don't like. It's in the South.

(Later.) I'm sitting around a table with a lot of people and we're cracking nuts—walnuts. I think we're inside a barn. I'm old. Never remarried. My son's right here. He's strong. I think he's a carpenter.

(Sounds like you're proud of him.) Very.

(Preceding death.) I'm in the house and I'm very sick. I'm in the bed. My son and his wife are there. I can see the graveyard from my window, see the old stones. I'm kind of scared. Someone is cooking in the kitchen. I can smell the food. They cook in big black copper pots. The kids are playing in the house, too. I'm eighty-nine.

(After the death.) I'm inside of a tree. I'm nothing. Yeh, I can see the body. They're with it. I feel happy.

(You love your trees and your nature, don't you?) Yes.

(What was the lesson?) Loss. Loss of my wife.

(Go to another lifetime that is impacting your life today.) I'm at some kind of resort like the Riviera, some gauche resort. It's the 1920's. I'm lying on a beach in a

bikini. [In those days?] There's a beautiful umbrella next to me in the sand so I won't get too tan. There are waiters bringing drinks to us. I have a sexy body. I'm nineteen.

(Later.) I'm dancing. I can't figure what it's all about. We're at some kind of club. I have on a lot of jewels, a string of pearls and things on my hands. I'm still nineteen.

(Are you dancing with anyone important?) Yes. I just know he's going to propose to me soon. He's very handsome, charming with dark hair and dark eyes.

(Is he familiar?) Yes. I think it's my husband now?

(Later.) We're at a picnic on a hillside, my husband and I. We have two kids. I'm twenty-five. There's white linen, champagne, strawberries, silver, etc. There's a nanny taking care of the kids. I don't have full responsibility for them. It's a family picnic.

(Later.) There's some problems. My husband is Russian and for some reason we're ostracized from our society. I think it's because he's Russian. He tells me about the war and the revolution. He chose to leave. He was very, very rich. His mother is still alive in Russia. He brought out a lot of his wealth. His stories sparked my interest.

(Later.) We're walking on the street and it's cold and snowy. The children are tenish. We're bundled up—it's cold. We're very happy. We learned something about being ostracized. I think we're going to church. I think we are in Russia because it's a big round church. I'm not sure. We're inside the church and we're walking in and sitting down. People are poor there. There's no seats. We have to bring

Alive Again...Again...and Again

*our own chairs. There's a stage at the end. It's a big cav-
ernous building. Someone is talking about poverty, food
and cold.*

*(Did you come to hear the speaker?) Yes. It's his broth-
er, actually. He's trying to organize and unite the people.*

*(Are you speaking to the brother?) No. We're rich. He
doesn't want to be seen speaking to us. He will talk to us
later, in a tiny house—not like our house in France. He and
his mother are there (in the tiny house). They have nothing.
They don't care. They are happy the way they are. There's
good feelings. They love the children.*

*(Later.) It's a hot day and we're in the fields. I have on
an old dress. My children are much older now—actually
adults. We're picking corn. I feel strong. My body is in
good shape. Birds are there, large ones, big black ones. He's
at home and I'm going back to the house now. It's an old
barn, nothing special. He's at a typewriter. He's writing.
When we make love, we're very much in love. He's writing
something very important—it's about the revolution. I
can't see the title. He supports it. He gave up everything
and came back.*

*(Later.) I'm at a pool and I'm with my mother. I'm at a
pool at a country club. We're sitting, drinking some drinks
in the sun. I'm in my forties. She's a neat lady. She's supportive in her own way. She lives somewhere in America.
She's American. I think my father wasn't there. I think he
left her. C_____ L____(a known name).*

(Are you going back to Russia soon?) No, not soon.

Alive Again...Again...and Again

(Do you miss your husband?) Yeh.

(Later.) It's really bad. We're in a terrible car crash. It's in Europe on a big highway. My husband and I, we both died. We're in our forties or fifties.

(Did you do any writing?) I helped him, that's all (in this lifetime she is a reporter).

(Do you see husband's spirit, also?) Yes.

(Has anyone come for you?) Not for a long time. Very desolate there. I'm going up toward the sun. He's behind me.

(Anyone coming to greet you?) Yes. A really nice energy.

(What was the lesson?) Respect for human beings, people over material wealth.

(Move to that higher level of consciousness, to what we call High Self.)

(Skills being used in this lifetime?) No. Just the experience. Respect and how political structures work.

Possibly these were two lifetimes experienced by the same person. They were completely different experiences. The amount of wealth was just another one of the features of any given life. **The wealth has nothing to do with the soul or the core person. Circumstances of the lifetimes were merely the stage on which the scene was set.** Both of the personalities in the previous regressions had great dignity. They knew who they were and were true to their principles.

Alive Again...Again...and Again

Trappings of the physical did not control their actions.

That brings us back to the bank's automatic teller window. An ego functioning at the middle-ego level would probably perceive that it's alright to keep the $200.00 because there's a group tape that is something like, "You've got to take what you can. If you don't, someone else will." How many times have you heard from someone that an activity is acceptable because "everyone else is doing it?"

High-ego has started to analyze the experiences of life and is allowing the awareness of the soul or Spirit to influence conclusions. High-ego tends not to take "group tapes" as truth and starts to look for the justice in any given situation. **"Group tapes" are very subtle, sometimes, and the high-ego does not always recognize a program as "defective." A defective tape or a defective program, as in a computer, would be one that does not always give reliable results.** Perhaps there was a mistake in the logic that developed the program. For example, look at the tape that says, "success is measured by money." Are not some of the most miserable people you know wealthy? What is success? Maybe they are not successful, they just have money. Then, we jump to the opposite tape that says, "money is the root of all evil." But, do you not also know or know of people who have wealth, but are also happy and do much good with their money? Yet, many who function at a high-ego level have a problem with money because they accept some of the money tapes but may reject others.

Each of these levels contributes to our growth. **To be able to function at a level in which all tapes are recognized and analyzed for the components of "truth and justice" would be beyond the level of the ego.** Besides, some tapes are not

significant to a person in a given lifetime. How busy we
would be if we had to analyze tapes all the time? Certain
tapes may pertain to a particular individual or group in a
specific lifetime. Triggering mechanisms that occur at birth
or at other significant times in a lifetime may bring up a particular tape or tapes.

**Ego is connected to the physical. It is the filter through
which the soul observes the lessons of life in the physical.**
To eliminate ego, which some religious systems would have
us do, would negate much of the learning and understanding and wisdom available from fully embracing the life one
is experiencing. **There will be eons of times to be experienced as a soul, or Spirit, without the physical dimensions;
but only during those privileged times when a soul comes
into physical incarnation on this beautiful planet earth can
it learn those lessons unique to this medium. You are truly
fortunate and blessed to be here, especially at this time of
"accelerated growth."**

A Time of Accelerated Growth

Why do I call this a time of accelerated growth? As you
read the regressions, pay attention to the number of lessons
or the kinds of experiences available in any given lifetime. In
today's world, you may record in one week as many experiences as others, in centuries past, may have recorded in an
entire lifetime. Every time you see a newscast or watch a
movie or read a novel, you may experience a wide range of
emotions. **One might suggest that improved communication has increased the efficiency with which one gathers
information and experiences in the more recent lifetimes.** If
you are able to analyze your reactions and acquire some kind

of understanding or wisdom, and see the truth and justice in those experiences, so much the better. Which experiences push your buttons? Ah. Good information about yourself and, therefore, others.

MORE ABOUT ADDICTION

What of our addicts? What did we know of addictions in earlier times? People were judged and condemned to live and die with their addictions. Now we see beyond the addiction to the "core person." Addicted people are able to move through and manage the addiction, if they choose, and, consequently, gain understanding and wisdom that before may have taken lifetimes to acquire. **Consider the possibility that an addiction is really a mirror of our own culture?** Have these people agreed to come here and experience their addictions to show us what the weaknesses are in our culture? **There is no way to escape from being forced to look at your own life if you have an addicted person in the family or working with you. Learning experiences are forced on you whether you want them or not.**

Earlier we talked about "group tapes." Does "buying into" those "group tapes" lead to addictions such as alcohol abuse, sex abuse, work abuse, racism, extreme nationalism, preoccupations with money and violence, or other activities that do not contribute to the highest good of the individual, the family, or the society? On the other hand, if learning is occurring—though it may be in a difficult way—maybe those behaviors are contributing to the highest good.

If so, you are living in a time when there is great opportunity for change. You can look at the soul's history—your own and/or others—and clean up the no longer useful "tapes" you may be carrying in your "computer." You can look at the culture's history and collectively clean up the defective "tapes" or "programs" in that "computer." **We become a metaphor for the clearing of the pollution we have caused earth as we clean up our own polluted thought patterns. The cleansing of Mother Earth becomes a metaphor for our own cleansing.**

Remember who you are. Look for the truth and justice in any given situation. What is the truth and does it mean justice or fairness for all involved? Evaluate tapes and experiences. Dare to stand up and speak out for what you perceive to be untruth and injustice. Treasure your ego-centrics for they often are not of a "groupthink" or middle-ego mentality. They often dare to challenge the status quo and may have a message for all. That is not to say that you would agree with them, but that you would value their right to be heard and their bravery for being willing to stand up for their beliefs. Remember the times in history when one person made a difference. Among those who may qualify as egocentrics who made a difference are Moses, Jesus, Gandhi, Thomas Paine, Galileo, Columbus, and the list goes on.

The following regression is about a man who dared to stand up against the establishment, the group-think, and by all appearances lost everything. However, in the grander scheme of things, our society gained a lasting reward from his bravery.

(Where are you?) It's a brick building, big and tall. It's hard to see the sky. I am wearing shoes and the road is cobblestone. The shoes are leather, clunky, slip-ons. It's burned out! It's not a surprise. There's great, great sadness. It's my

home and it's not there anymore. It's gutted. It sits on a corner. It's not like the whole city was destroyed. A fire-bomb. Somebody did it. And, my family, wife and kids, are gone. I'm male, about 35. I was out. Politics. London.

(Go to a time when you were expressing your views.) I was talking to a crowd of people about starting child labor laws, keeping kids out of the factories. They're listening, but they're afraid because of how powerful the mill owners are. They want to do something. They are threatened by the mill owners. I don't work in the factories. I'm an aristocrat. That's why I'm effective because the people who work in the factories listen to me. They think I'm powerful enough to do something.

(Later.) I have an image of coming down the steps and people are lined up looking at me like I'm a hero. Looks like I'm coming out of a courthouse. I think I got the laws changed. After the loss of my family, I didn't have a lot to lose. It was my dad (in this lifetime) who burned out my house and killed my family. He was aristocracy. He owned them or something. Part of it was jealousy because I was too happy. I had two children.

(Go back to a time when you were with the wife and children.) I'm just coming home and they've been playing and laughing. They're happy to see me. My wife is there, too; she's been playing with them. There's a lightness and joy.

(Go to the time preceding your death.) I'm not old. I'm in a dark, damp room facing the window and praying. The window is dirty and doesn't let in much light. It's prison. Feels like all I tried to do was do the right thing and yet I kept getting hurt. I lost everything. Some people trumped

up some charges. I've been here for days. They just brought me there and I'm trying to figure out what happened. I'm praying to God for guidance. I made a lot of enemies and they're just out to get me. It doesn't matter what I've done.

There seems to be an extreme amount of injustice in all this. They are going to execute me. They are not doing this out in the light. It's not being done legally. It's just a bunch of people who've abducted me. It's like a lynching. I have a manacle around my neck. They take me out in the court-yard and shoot me. It's not civilized. They have laws and courts run by a group of people who are very powerful.

They put the body in a beggar's grave. I feel alone, alone, alone. The poor people may inquire, but they don't have any power. And, that's that.

(After the death.) I'm still with the body. It's like there's nowhere else to go. I just think I'm all by myself. I stay a couple of years. I just stay there in the body being dead. There was this big bright light. Then, I follow the light and everything lightens up. I'm joyful and peaceful. There are people who care. There they are.

(What happened after your death?) The laws stayed in effect. They saved the other children at the expense of my own.

*(Lesson.) I came to save the children. **But I don't know what lesson I learned—maybe that what seems like injustice on the small scale, on the large scale is not.***

(Is there a message from High Self?) Be happy.

Alive Again...Again...and Again

This person was one who still has a strong sense of justice in the present life. In fact, she is often saddened by the injustice she sees and finds it difficult to be happy. As a promoter of child labor laws in England, the influence of this individual who dared to stand up for truth and what he perceived to be injustice, is still being felt today. **In the grander scheme of things, society gained from this soul having come into that lifetime to fight for the rights of children.**

Learn from your history, both present and past lifetimes; learn from the history of others; and learn from world history. **Not to continually repeat the mistakes of the past is growth.** In the next regression, we see a man who tapped into a lifetime as an **Native American** Indian and found that the experiences of that lifetime have been profoundly affecting his present life. His story and the knowledge he wanted to share from that lifetime follow.

(Describe the vegetation along the path.) There's grass. I'm wearing sort of shoes, mocassins. There are tepees. The family is there. There's no fire. We're eating a stew. There's Father and Mother. I'm twenty-one and a male. There are four or five brothers and sisters. I'm the oldest son.

(Later.) There's a battle. I'm in it. I'm on horse. It's with white men in uniforms. There are so many. So many come. Too many. I have a gun and a tomahawk and a knife. I must fight. Many Indians are in the battle.

(Preceding death.) Not on a horse. A bullet in the chest. I'm lying in a creek or river. I fell into the river. The river was nearby. My head is barely out of the water.

(Do you still see the body?) No. It's wrapped in robes.

Alive Again...Again...and Again

My family, they grieve for me. I'm not married. Not many died. Sioux. Battle was successful against them. Several chiefs. All the white men were killed. It was called "greasy grass." That's what we called it.

(Is it Little Big Horn?) I think so.

(Is your body to be cremated?) No. It's put on a scaffold so Spirit will rise to the Great Father. Body is on the scaffold. I see a very loving Father welcoming me home.

(Lesson.) I died for something I really didn't believe in. I couldn't understand it.

(The killing?) Yes. Maybe the hatred. Maybe that's why I got killed—not being as good a warrior as others. I saw many friends killed and soldiers.

(You didn't want to kill?) Indian teaching. The Indian ways, I miss them. It means so much. Man doesn't know what he's doing today. It will all come to pass. The trail may be . . . (he paused) but, I believe I had to fight, but afterwards it seemed such a waste. Killing was terrible. Slaughter. I probably welcomed death at that time. Perhaps I willed it. I wasn't very proud. It could have been a bullet from another warrior. There was much confusion. I loved my family. I think my son (in present life) was somebody in that family.

Compassion. Understanding. Love. It would be so different in the world today.

(Can you use the Indian teachings and ways to impact the world today?) There must be. I want to find it. The love

that I felt from the Great Spirit, I'll never forget. I want to love other people as He loved me.

(Is there much of the Indian spirit in the life today?) Yes. It is there. We make great teachers—spiritual teachers. I'll never forget that. Today, people make fun and laugh. We were lovers of everything. Everything has spirit. It was a wonderful time.

(So you truly understood the meaning of the oneness?) Yes. Very much so. Even Indians today have lost contact with the old ways and they die on the reservations. It saddens my heart to see it.

But . . . I died brave. We must get back to the Great Spirit or all is lost.

(What is the greatest danger?) **Man's ignorance. His denial of Higher Beings. Raping of the earth. I just speak from the heart.**

The Indian lifetime is greatly impacting this man's life today. He seems to have an understanding of the Indian belief system and plans to use that understanding to help heal the earth and the people who are destroying her.

REMEMBER WHO YOU ARE

Remember who you are and why you are here. **You are Spirit in the physical.** Taking $200.00 from the bank that is not yours does not contribute to your reason for being. Stand up for who you are and dare to stand up for something meaningful and valuable. A word of caution is in order. Even as you dare to stand up for what you believe to be an accurate perception of the world, you must also recognize the right of others to stand up for their perceptions. Our perceptions may not agree. **These differing perceptions are more opportunities for growth which contribute to that diversity of experience available to us all.**

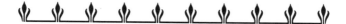

Alive Again...Again...and Again

Chapter V

Power

What is power? **It would appear to be the ability to influence your own environment for the development and nurturing of yourself and those in your care.** Power is an issue that seems to come up more for women because men seem to accept power and use it with more comfort. Men also seem to have more of it or the appearance of having more of it. Reconciling issues around power, and the differences in perceived power based on male or female incarnations, is necessary. Our culture and most others also support power for men. Women in cultures even less enlightened than our own need to resolve issues around power in order to feed and clothe their children and control the number of children that they have. For other women, especially career-oriented women, critical issues concerning power are present in the workplace. They are not comfortable with it and are not sure how to use it. My work with women and their power issues has revealed some real cultural biases that are very old. **There are also cultural biases that limit the power of men, such as poverty, disability, and ethnic origin.**

Alive Again...Again...and Again

Notice that we have not defined power as having to do with control over others. This notion is a perception supported by our culture, but it is not relevant to the discussion of power presented here. **We are talking about the perception of individuals that they have some influence over the events and environment that are part of their lives, including their own bodies.**

FORGIVENESS

Ironically, one of the most successful ways to regain your power is to forgive those who have taken it. In the cases of rape, incest, abuse, and other assaults on ones power over the self, forgiving the perpetrator is useful in the process of "working through" the issues caused by assaults on individual self-power. To accomplish this kind of forgiveness requires a world view that sees individuals as souls who are greater than the facade presented in the physical. **Never is forgiveness confused with accepting unacceptable behaviors.** You are able to forgive another while, at the same time, rejecting the behavior. Much growth is achieved when forgiveness is accomplished. It is not an easy thing to do. Later regressions in this chapter will deal with those physical assaults on your power.

In the first two regressions, a professional woman was struggling with male/female issues around power and leadership. She had a fear of being ineffective unless she emulated the male role. We asked for a couple of lifetimes to give us insight into effectiveness as a male leader and then as a female leader. The stories were disturbing.

(Describe what you see.) There's grass, like lawns. I feel a house. It's large and light. There's a sense of contemporary furniture. There's a sense of a lot of people. There's a big man in particular. He's kindly. I think a father.

It's a party. I think I'm small. Everyone's big. I'm watching them dance. I get a sense this is a long time ago. There's a cottage. It's big, like a fairytale. Seems more like peasantry. They're happy. Just a sense of looking up. The big man's there. I get a sense of my mother. More women are dancing than men.

(Later.) There's a meeting. I feel about the same. At a table. The big man is at the head of the table. The room is darker. There's a fireplace. There's mostly men there. I don't see women. It's intense. I'm standing on the floor. I have a sense it's political. The big man is in charge of it. The rebellion. I think that's what they're planning. Seems like we're either English or American. Seems like it's very intense and has to do with them being poor. There's some discussion of land—ownership. The meeting lasts into the night.

(Later.) I have a sense I'm older now and I think I'm a guy. I'm hunting. I'm starting to see myself with boots on, leather clothing, vests. Hunting game. I enjoy it. I like being outside. It's the fall. I hunt alone. No horse. I walk. I bring it home for food. I sense I'm in my late teens. I'm strong, healthy, very strong. It's nice.

(Move to another significant event.) I'm getting married. We're dancing. We go arm in arm like waltzing, but not waltzing. Just the two of us dancing. She's blonde with curly hair. It's quite a party. I think we're in a cottage again. I sense a lot of people in a small place. We're drinking out

*of tankards. Drinking and feasting. Everyone's dancing.
The table they had at their meeting is off to the side. The
cottage is big, but not divided up into rooms. It's very
happy. Very jovial. The big man is happy. I think I'm his
only son. In fact, I don't get a feeling that I have brothers
and sisters. Sense a stronger connection to the father. Party
goes into the night. We drink and dance. Some get very
drunk. But, all having fun still. I think my bride is very
young. I don't think we know each other that well. We're
both shy. We have like a loft in that cottage. The ladder is
off to the side.*

*(Another significant event.) My wife's had a baby. She
looks tired, but she and the baby seem to be doing okay. She
has the baby in arms. It's daytime. We're not in the loft
anymore. We're in a sunnier room with windows. I think
it's a baby boy. I'm very excited. The big man is there, too.
He's very excited. There's a real connection between the
two of them. She's fine. She's nursing. I don't get a sense of
my mother being here anymore. The baby is blonde. I have
dark hair. He looks like my wife.*

*(Later.) I'm an old man. I'm sitting at a table. It seems
like a meeting again, but I'm at the head of the table. It's at
night again and again it's only men. Political. It seems like
it's a continuation of before, but in a different direction. It
has to do with trade. It seems like I'm wealthier than my
father was and these people are business men. They are
traders. There's no women. We're talking about laws and
restrictions to trade, and they're angry because they are
being restricted. I'm the leader. I get a sense we're in
America. The discussion seems to revolve around England.
We're very angry. I think we're near a seaport. I see ships
and references to sailing ships as part of this discussion.*

There's a sense of secrecy about this meeting.

(Preceding death.) I'm in a bed. By myself. I'm old. I look sick and skinny. The vitality is gone.There's a candle by the bed. I feel like I'm looking at myself from above, but I'm still alive. I have on a nightshirt. It's an old-fashioned bed and I am going to die. That's okay. In fact, I'm leaving right now. I'm sensing heat when I'm moving upwards. I see gold colors. I feel great. Airy, light, floating. I'm surrounded by light. I get a sense that there are friends around me, but I don't see anything. On the other side of the Light, they are welcoming me—telling me to rest. It's great.

(Lesson?) Has to do with the big man. He and I needed to work on our relationship—understand each other. Also, to continue to discover the role of leadership. It was a good life.

(Why were women never involved?) **It truly seems that they were never of any consequence.** *They fed us, gave us children. They were a support unit of our cause. The relationship between men seemed to be the focus no matter what that relationship was. It was just expected that they would take care of the men, period. I don't have a sense of a connection with my child—not really.*

(What would happen if women didn't do for the men?) Never experienced it.

(Move to that higher level of consciousness, to what we call the High Self.)

(What is the purpose of showing this lifetime?) Political. A discussion of involvement. A lesson in involvement and

leadership. Sense a fighting of the leadership role. Pushing it away, too.

(Fear?) Too masculine. It seems like that's how I was when I was a leader. **When I was a leader, I was male. Seems to be difficulty translating that to female. Stuck between the two.**

(Go back to another time when you were a leader and female.) Inside. Get a sense of a church. I'm speaking to a group of people. I have blonde hair. Again, this seems political. It's men and women. I'm speaking. I'm very emotional. Pleading with them to do something, to listen. I'm waving my arms for emphasis. Pleading, not in a begging way, but more authoritative way. I have a scarf on my head attached to the hair. Again, it's night time. I'm about thirty. Like a few pews filled. Feel like I'm dressed in blue, but not a nun. I'm dressed average—borderline peasant. It's like I'm pleading for someone's life, someone on trial. I'm asking them to listen to me about this person. I sense I'm pleading for a child, a young person. The crowd isn't listening. I visualize myself in blue and everyone else is in black. Faceless. I know there's men and women because of their hats. They're very cold. Their minds are made up and closed. I knew this when I started talking to them. Feels like I'm more in a courtroom, a hearing. More like a town hall. No "God" things around.

(What is happening?) They are angry with me. I'm not afraid. They're mad. They think I'm a little crazy. I have a sense it has to do with witchcraft. It's just a child. They don't care. It's not my child. I don't have any children.

(Later.) I feel like there's another meeting. There's a

mob. We're actually at an execution. They're angry. It's a little girl they are going to execute. She's eight or nine. I see the little girl. She's frightened. She doesn't even know why. I think she's mentally ill—deaf or mute or something and they don't understand why. And . . . I know her somehow. I don't get a sense of her parents. I get a sense of a little street urchin that I befriended. I'm a single woman. She has to climb scaffolding—stairs above. I think they are going to hang her. I'm shouting, but no one cares. They're shouting, too, for different reasons. I can't watch this. I don't understand how they can be so mad at a little girl. I keep yelling, "She's just a little girl." I sense they don't understand her—afraid of her. They're afraid of her being there. There are a lot of people here. I have an attachment to her, but not as mother and child.

(Following execution.) She's cut down and thrown into a grave. I go and put flowers by it. I feel really bad. I feel like I have to apologize for everybody. I think I knew that little girl. I think she's my Grandma (in the present life). She was an orphan. I felt the people were "ignorant."

(Death.) I'm in bed. Old. I'm dressed in black. I'm looking at myself. I don't think I ever married. It seems I lived a fairly solitary existence. I feel like I'm just dying of old age. Seems to be the way it is and always has been—to be by myself. I'm starting to join them. Gold Light. Died.

(Is the little girl there?) Yes. She's happy to see me. I don't think she's mad. She does understand.

(Are you feeling some responsibility for not being able to save her?) Yes. She says it wasn't my responsibility. She loves me.

Alive Again...Again...and Again

(Move to a higher level of consciousness, to what we call the High Self.)

(Is there a leadership issue here with men and women? Failed?) **Fear of being ineffective unless she follows the male roles. Unable to bridge that. Fear of being ineffective as a female and being an overpowering male leader. A balance. Fear failure to give guidance and fear of over-guidance.**

(Will she be able to accomplish this balance?) Eventually. Could be outside of work. Probably outside of work. Fear of loss.

(Is there a message?) Patience.

Because of our attitudes toward females when we are males, we often set ourselves up to experience a restricted life as a female. The client who experienced the previous regressions as a male did not think women had value except to have children and to serve their husbands. As a woman, she experienced a powerlessness. The story that follows is from a client who does not have confidence in her ability to learn. She describes herself as a slow learner. She comes from a family of high-achievers and has brothers who are very successful. To build her confidence I asked that she go back to a time when it was easy for her to learn and to express her-self. Notice what thought patterns are revealed.

(What are you experiencing?) I feel like I'm a man. I'm a teacher. I'm teaching health, nutrition, and philosophy. I was a philosopher. It was easy.

(Was it as easy for all your students?) No. I feel like I

was patient, holding them in my arms and reassuring. I had a lot of love for those students. There were good feelings between each other. I was a teacher the whole time. It feels good. It feels rewarding. I traveled. I went where I wanted. I was single and enjoyed the freedom. Very carefree.

I felt I could understand when it was difficult to learn. Everyone has to learn at his own rate. I let them come after school for help if they needed it. I feel like I had knickers on. 1900. Joseph. New York. I died at fifty-two.

I was happy with my work, but I wasn't happy with women. I see myself with a lot of women—like a bar scene—kind of playfully hitting them on the fanny. I didn't want to get involved in any relationship. The students were all boys. **I didn't think women were as intelligent as men.** *Women weren't allowed to show their intelligence. They were just to be housewives and playmates. I may have taken advantage of women. I think I used them. That's why I'm being used now.*

(Preceding death.) I see a woman standing over my bed crying. My lover. I did have a relationship. I loved this woman very much and I felt badly about leaving her. I was dying and leaving her. I'm dying of a weak heart. **Only later in life did I learn to love. That's why my heart was weak.**

(After death.) I see a lot of White Light. I came to learn to have compassion and love for other people and to teach them good things. In the preceding life, **I feel like I have learned to have compassion for others, but I haven't really learned to love. There's a possible connection between learning problems and old beliefs.**

Alive Again...Again...and Again

As a male, she believed women were less intelligent than males and then, in this lifetime, as a female, she found learning difficult. Perceptions of powerlessness and weakness are just as restricting as physical limitations. **These attitudes toward women are found in many cultural experiences**. One woman who was working with feelings of anger for men went back to a lifetime in a Native American culture. Her frustration is apparent.

> *(Where are you?) I'm outside. It's a flat area jutting out of a cliff wall. It goes straight down. I live there. Much sacrifice. I'm like a cliff dweller. I'm a child, female. We're Anasazi Indians. We're short people. I see a mother with lots of little children.*

> *(Later.) It looks like an Indian chief, from the colors of the robes and feathers, standing on the edge of the cliff. He's gazing off into the distance. I think he's our leader. We do all the work and he gets all the credit for being such a great leader.*

> *(Later.) I see the very narrow little ledge and Indian braves walking along it. It's very dangerous. It seems like I'm this generic woman running around trying to keep these kids under control, while they go out and wear war paint and pretty clothes and do exciting things. It's like I'm kind of frantic with no clear sense of purpose, while it's pretty clear what they have to do. I envy their clear sense of purpose, to participate in this dance and do this feat or ritual of some kind. They have a clarity and I just buzz, buzz, buzz. The old chief just looks out and sees visions of the future. They don't seem to worry about survival issues; I seem to be doing all the work. It seems like corn is grown. Men help, too, with food. It must be the higher echelon who*

don't help. They dream and dance. They're selected by lineage. They get privileges.

(How do women fit into this?) Workers.

(What about the very bright woman?) She's just resentfully grinding her corn.

(What if she has visions?) **They're never asked.**

In the previous regression the woman felt undervalued and powerless. In another culture, a woman experiences a total lack of control of her life even though she has the trappings of power. Would that not create confusing thought patterns around power? Imagine the confusing issues around power that could come out of the following scenario.

(Where are you?) It's a place lined with elephant tusks. It's like making an archway to walk through. It's like a ceremony. It's a special area. I'm privileged, I'm special. It's just the way it is. I'm female and I'm wearing a white gown. The elephant tusks are like a protection for me.

(Are you like a queen?) Yes. [Sounds good so far!] I have dark skin and I live in a large building. Everything is very large like a lot of marble. There's a large room inside. There's a stairway in the entry. My bedroom is very ornate, but not gaudy. There is a lot of velvet. I have a dressing table, a large bed with a canopy, and tall ceilings. I'm twenty-five.

(Move to the time of the main meal.) I stand behind the king. I'm not at the table. There are just men at the table. I eat in the kitchen. I also have to serve them. I do more like

entertaining and serving, pour the wine, things like that.

(Is the king your age?) No. He's older.

(Do you love him?) No. I'm more like a servant. I'm his wife, but I serve him. I'm not his first wife. There were others, but they were killed. Their time was served. None of them had children.

(He has the power to have them killed?) Yes. I have not served him long. If he doesn't like them anymore or gets mad at them, he can have them killed. You had to marry him if selected. I was just a regular person. He saw me in the streets.

(Are you beautiful?) Yes. **I knew others had been killed. It's an honor.**

(Even if you may die?) Yes.

(Later.) We're outdoors. We're making an announcement. We're going to have a child. He's happy.

(Later.) Something's not right. I'm sick. I'm having a lot of pain. Miscarrying. He doesn't want to know. I don't tell him. I just try again. He thinks I'm still pregnant. I think he stabs me when he finds out. It's like I defied him. He stabbed me in the chest. I don't die immediately.

(Does he stay?) Yes. He's sorry, in a selfish way. He won't have me anymore. He stays till I die. He's just sitting there. Just sad. He seems familiar.

(What was the lesson in that lifetime?) **That being**

obedient wasn't really what I should do. That was not really the right kind of life.

(Move to that higher level of consciousness, to what we call the High Self.) She's trying to be obedient.

(Is that not right for her again?) No. She needs to be creative.
(Is she afraid to be?) Yes.

(Why?) Finances. She needs to make a living.

(Is there a message for her?) Change direction.

Another woman was instructed to return to a lifetime in which she really felt her power. When threatened with the loss of her power she took extreme measures. **This young woman was feeling powerless in nearly every aspect of her present life, and I wanted her to experience the energy of feeling power within herself.** The scenario was a little surprising. Perhaps I should have omitted the adverb "really" from the instructions. So, what follows is a time when she **really** felt her power.

(What is happening?) There is a storm and I have summoned it. I feel wind rushing through my hair and robe. There's lightning and thunder. I feel at one with the storm.[This was said with much force and strength.]

(Did you need the rain?) No. I did not need the rain. I just did it for the fun of it—just to feel my own power. [She spoke with such depth, volume, and authority that I was quite amazed. The client was a very soft-spoken, petite blonde, and to hear these powerful words thundering

out of her was a unique experience for me.]

(Is that acceptable?) To me it is. It doesn't matter what other people think. I'm proud and I am free and I do what I will. I am female. I scorn men and their paltry little attempts to control me. I will be no man's slave. I have my inheritance and I have my servants. I don't mind doing things for myself. Our culture values women. We are Celts. We see the invaders from the south bringing their sky gods who seek to enslave women in marriage.

(How do you stay safe from invaders?) We have warriors among us—men and women. Fortunately they have not come close enough to threaten us. They get closer each year. I treat my servants well—there are only a few—as long as they leave me to my chambers. My home is small, but adequate.

(Preceding death.) I'm in my home. The invaders have come. I will not bow to their ways. I will not bow to their customs. They seek to force me. They want to try to make me do what they want, but I will have the last say. I drive the spear into my heart. I will not live the life they force on me. They were very surprised. They are used to having their way with women.

(After the death?) I hover above the body looking down. I see them gaping down at the body and complaining that I have deprived them of fine spoil.

(What was the lesson to be learned in that lifetime?) To be strong. To follow my heart .To be strong about what I believe in. To be willing to die rather than give up my conviction.

Alive Again...Again...and Again

Her solution is certainly not recommended for others, but this client was feeling powerless in her present life and needed to tap into a time when she felt strong.

Few cultures on our planet, at least historically, have supported the autonomy of women. Through regressions, many cultures have been visited and rarely do the women have any power. Unfortunately, that sense of a lack of power seems to stay with souls when they are in a female incarnation. Most of those who accept the philosophy of reincarnation believe that souls incarnate in both male and female bodies. Therefore, females cannot say that male souls are to blame for this unfortunate attitude because, as we have seen in some earlier examples, when some souls take on the male body, they buy into the same attitudes toward women. **There appear to be lessons to be learned as a "soul-group" about mutual respect and equality.** Another culture, whose attitudes toward women are less than equitable, is represented in the regression that follows.

(Describe the vegetation along the path.) The path is pebbles. There's trees and slender bamboo. It's an oriental garden. There's a pond with some lily pads and Koi fish. I have on a kimono and slippers with button-on shoes. I'm female and fourteen. The gardens are more extensive than for an ordinary house. They are our gardens. The house is all wood—natural wood. It has the screen doors. There are three stairs, then a ledge or balcony around the house and then another two steps up and then you go inside the screen. There is a low black table that has a real simple flower arrangement.

(Is anyone with you?) I don't know if it's my mother or a helper. Outside there's a round black hot rack that is like

a barbecue. The fish are on sticks. She's bringing them in to a table. It's a larger rectangular black table. There's a man at one end of the table, my brother, who is about my age. The women serve the men, including my brother, and then sit down on the knees. Everything is done in a ritual—even the way the meal is eaten. It's like everything is very controlled and calm and passive.

(Later.) My father is leaving. He is a General or some type of military official. He has to go to some conflict. He's going away because of his position and my brother is taking over the household. I'm not excited about that. I fear him. My mother needs to be submissive to him, also. We must be very isolated. I don't see any friends. I spend a lot of time in the garden. He's cold and cruel. Egotistical. I'm not afraid of my father—he shows a good front, but he's soft and caring. I'm not afraid he won't come back, but he'll be gone a long time. I think he knows how I feel about my brother, but he's also proud of my brother.

(Later.) I'm outside again in the garden and there's a full moon and I'm running away. My mother knows this and is helping me. I'm staying with some relatives of my mother's so I have a place to go. It's because of my brother. I don't see that he's done anything to harm me. He's controlling everything in my life. Everything I do is criticized and judged by him. I don't take to heart what he says. It's just that it is so negative and so rigid.

(Later.) I am learning flower arranging and drawing. It's a type of art class environment. It's wonderful because that is what I wanted to do, but wasn't allowed to do. I'm in a small fishing-type village. It's much more positive.

Alive Again...Again...and Again

My brother is there looking for me. He has found out where I am. I'm hiding and I can hear him. He's saying he'll find me and bring me back. When I think of him, it's like a big black cloud. I can't understand why he would want to hurt me so much. I think it's a blow to his male ego. It must be hard for mother, but it was a gift that she gave me even though she knew the remainder of her time with him would be hard.

Everything about the village I like except missing my mother. There's more to do work-wise. I have friends there, too. There's a lot more freedom in everything. In my own home everything was very controlled. Here there is a lot more feeling and talking and laughing.

(Later.) I have a really good friend and I'm trying to decide what to do—either keep running or enter some kind of order. I can't become a Buddhist priest as a woman, but something like that. I want one so that your life is spent something like in a monastery, but focuses on the arts. I wouldn't be able to see my friend again or my mother and father. I'd have no contact at all. The only thing I wouldn't have to give up would be the art. I decide to go to it. There doesn't seem to be a problem with giving up the idea of being married. There must not be anyone interesting in the village.

(Later.) I've somehow found out—I don't know how—that my mother had died and that it wasn't just recently, but a while ago. I'm sitting by a pond. It's smooth and I drop in a pebble and say this is my gift to you and the rings come out of the pebble. I drop it in real gently. I have the feeling that what she gave to me, the small ring, grows larger and larger. It's a larger gift and it keeps growing.

Alive Again...Again...and Again

The good friend that I had in the village, her energy is my mother's energy now.

*(Later.) I'm drawing. What I've just done I really like and it's very simple. It's a drawing of a very simple flower arrangement. It's actually like a watercolor. Every time I start to think about my brother my good feelings get squashed. I am still thinking about him. **I don't feel any love there, just power.** Lot of anger from him about me.*

(Preceding death) I'm outside. I kill myself by stabbing myself with a knife. I'm in my twenties or thirties.

(Why?) Because the art loses out to my brother.

*(Lesson?) **To listen to my heart and the way I feel about it instead of the judgment and criticism of others. I was trying to learn to let go and didn't.***

Even though the brother was not with her, he still had power over her—over her thoughts. She could not escape him. Again, her method of escaping was consistent with that culture, but not acceptable in the present one. Escape, though not easy, is often possible in modern times. Frequently, options are not seen. She did not see any other options. **Today's woman must look for options for that is the art of problem solving—seeing options that are not readily apparent.**

RAPE

Rape is one of the most damaging traumas to the self and to your power. Rape not only threatens your life, but also your sense of power over your own body. Some of the clients who have returned to lifetimes when they were raped have found far-reaching effects in the present life. Two such examples follow.

(What is the vegetation like along the path?) It's a dirt and gravel road. There are like cornstalks beside it. There's some high vegetation. It seems like there's a farmhouse at the end of the road. It's kind of dark inside. It has a porch that goes all around with some pillars. There are rocking chairs. The walls inside look paneled. There's a dining room. I'm a little girl. Several kids are at the table. There's a mother and father and six kids. We're making lots of noise. It seems like we're dressed up, too, for dinner. I have on a velvet dress with a slip that makes it stick out. I'm around eight. A parasol keeps flashing like it's hot outside.

(Later.) Seems like we're outside hanging the wash up on the line, helping my mother. I see the boys coming out of the barn with the father and some cows. It seems like I might be the only girl and the rest are boys. It looks like I have on a blue and white checked dress with a white apron. It's to the ankles. I have on a hat and have two braids.

(Later.) We're all in the wagon like we're going into town for a dance or something. We're all dressed up. We're going to someone else's barn where we're having a party. There's music playing and people are dancing. There's a table with a bunch of food on it. Everyone brought some food. I'm ten. Kids are just spinning around. Kids are running in and out the door. Maybe it's a wedding. It might be the reception.

(Later.) I'm in a one-room schoolhouse and I'm the

teacher. I'm not that old—nineteen. I have maybe ten stu-
dents. There are old wood desks and I really like it.

(Later.) I see a smaller house by a stream or something.
I think that's where I live. It's all wood. It's not big at all.
It seems like there's a pump outside to pump water. There's
a lot of dirt, though. Dusty. I was outside pumping some
water and some people came up on horses. Three men. I
think I'm there by myself. I'm getting dragged into the
house. I'm fighting. It's violent. I'm raped by all three and
badly beaten up. I don't know if I died. It seems like they're
ransacking the house. It's almost like they're looking for
something. I think they're strangers. I think they're drink-
ing. They brought it (the alcohol). I didn't have it.

Now they're making food. There's two at the table and
one still with me. They are there a long time, laughing and
talking and having a good time. One has a gunbelt with
bullets across the chest and they have on hats that tie under
the chin. It seems like they're dirty and dusty. I don't know
if anyone's going to come out there. I must live alone. This
has gone on for awhile. I sense even till the next day.

(A few hours later.) They're talking about where
they're going. They want to find something. It's a long way
they have to go. I think they're leaving. They didn't kill
me—I'm still alive. I go into town to tell somebody. It
seems like I walked and it was a long way. My dress is all
ripped and my hair's a mess. The town doesn't look too big.
There are wood sidewalks. It's dusty. It seems like someone
comes out and grabs me and brings me into one of the
buildings. I tell them what happened. They're trying to get
a group together to go after them. There are some kids
around. They're crying because this happened to me.

Alive Again...Again...and Again

They're sitting at my feet. They're going out after them—five maybe.

(Later.) I see myself later on teaching school. Everyone knows what happened to me. It's different. I'm not happy in front anymore. I even stand different. I want to say I went back to my house and I shot myself—in my head.

(What was the lesson you came to learn?) No matter what they did to me I can come back. Won't let them get me down.

(Go to that higher level of consciousness, to what we call the High Self.)

(Is there physical trauma from that lifetime?) **Standoffish. Don't want anyone to get close. Get the chills when certain people touch me. Get all tight.**

(Anything from the bullet wound?) One eye. Get pain in one eye. Seems like that's where the bullet entered.

(Emotional trauma?) **Problem with people touching me that I don't want touching me. Bothers me a lot. I have to watch out all the time—on guard.**

(When in front of groups it's like everyone knows?) Yes. Like they're talking about me or something. Don't feel any of my family was around. Felt like there was no one I could talk to or tell. I don't think they knew. I think they knew after I died. **I feel like I wanted to talk to someone, but not to strangers so I felt all alone. Felt dirty around sex.**

(Mental trauma?) **Don't trust men a lot.** *I want my family to leave me alone a lot. It's like I don't want them to know what I'm doing. Maybe an embarrassment. I hate for people to stare at me. I don't like to go into a place by myself because I think everyone's looking at me. I'm bothered by dirty unshaven men.*

(Spiritual trauma?) **"Why me" comes up?** *What did I do wrong? Why is he punishing me? While rape was going on, I was asking God why He let me down?*

(Were you naive or innocent prior to that?) Yes. I usually operate like I don't need a lot of people around—that I can do it myself. Guess I need people.

(What about trust?) I have a hard time trusting men. Don't trust women either. The talking about me. It seems like they were talking about me when I came into town. Why me, still?

I was trying to do it by myself and they were married and didn't have to do it by themselves. Maybe I was jealous.

(And in this lifetime?) Still the thought to do it by myself in this lifetime.

Sometimes when I hear someone was raped I think, well, maybe they deserved it. Don't know why I think that. Don't think she (the girl in the regression) deserved it, but think other people did.

(Is there a message from the High Self?) **Need to let go of this.**

The knowledge that these events are affecting her life today has given her more power over her unexplained feelings. She is more trusting. She is more comfortable in front of groups. She is more comfortable with men. Ideally we would wish that this knowledge would immediately empower her and solve all her problems, however, as in most cases, life is much more complicated than that. While there are still many factors affecting her life, she experiences much growth and reclaims her power daily.

Another regression around rape involved a young woman who was having difficulty with her relationship with her father and with men. As you will see from the presence of "yucks" in the regression, she found this information nothing less than revolting.

> (Go to another lifetime when you were with the father.) Yuck. Gross. It's like we were lovers. I'm about eighteen with black hair in ringlets. This gives me the creeps. We're on the bridge. He's nuzzling me. A carriage is coming over. I feel the bridge is going to give way and I fall down into the rocks and splatter. Maybe he pushed me.

> (Go to an earlier time in that lifetime.) It's around 1813. I'm going down this old-timey street and the street is like mud. I'm going into the general store. I think my name is Sally Ann H. I'm coming out of the store. He's real debonair. Dapper clothes. He has a whip in his hands. He was like the playboy or catch of the town and I was kind of innocent and naive. I think I'm sixteen or seventeen. I didn't know that I was just like a conquest.

> I'm in our house and there are trees around. It's a southern feeling place. I sense Chattanooga. I think I'm

stalling. He starts coming by. I feel like there's a nanny and she knows he's no good. Of course, I don't see that. I was in the kitchen and he comes by. We go for a walk in the tall grass. He's undoing my bodice. He's prominent and I'm naive so I have a lot of fear associated with it. He rapes me fast. A hunter is close by and a gun goes off. He tosses me aside. I lay there crying. I'm ashamed. I think I lay there a good long while. I feel I also see the hunter. Feels like it was a woman wearing a cap—English hunting attire. Helen M.

My tears have dried. I'm thinking I have to go home. How am I going to get past everyone? I go to my room. I'm tormented inside. I get this kettle and I start scouring myself. I start crying all over.

(When do you see him?) I feel like I kind of hide out for awhile. I think that girl (the huntress) was a sister of his. I hide from her. The nanny is concerned. I don't sense any parents. I don't have anyone to turn to. I won't tell nanny.

(Later.) I feel like a roundness growing and nanny comes in to lace me up and she notices. She holds me and rocks me. She says we have to tell him and I'm just horrified because I know he'll laugh in my face. I tell him and he pushes me down in the dirt and whacks me with his whip and gets on his horse.

(Later.) He acts like he comes around and has me meet him on the bridge. He gets away with it. He says the carriage knocked me off balance. Nanny is the only one at my grave.

(What happens after your death?) I get the feeling she somehow got to work for his family and she poisoned him

because he killed her little girl.

(Move to that higher level of consciousness that we call the High Self.)

(Is there physical trauma?) Feels like such a wound to the belly because of the softness and the life that was in there. It was quick. Very rocky. There's a bruise on the right side of the head. That's probably what killed me. There was pain, too. It was a young virginal body and it didn't know what was happening. I wonder about kidneys. I was falling on stones and water was rushing beneath. I can see him up there. It just didn't affect him. He had no remorse. He was just getting me out of the way. **I've always known that I shouldn't have children in this lifetime.**

(Is there emotional trauma?) **A fear of intimacy and a fear of rejection. There's a fear of involvement and a fear of expression because look what happened when I told what was going on.** *This feels very good. Getting a strong picture of an eye. Seeing a lot. Some things will continue to unearth.*

(Mental patterns?) Fear of men. There's a definite fear of sexual involvement. **"When I am with a man, something bad will follow."**

(Spiritual level?) **The wounded body. I think that feels the saddest of all.**

(At this point I wanted her to tap into another lifetime when the experience of being with a man was positive to help balance the negativity experienced in the above lifetime.)

Alive Again...Again...and Again

(Go back to a time when being with a man was beautiful.) It's Medieval England time. He's like a Prince Charming. We have a little son and we're really happy.

(Experience completely feeling loved, valued and treasured.)

INCEST

Incest is another insidious form of sexual abuse that robs people of their power and sense of control over their lives. Traumas to the parts of the self can have a strong effect on the present life. For those who have experienced incest, what is most damaging is a loss of trust which results because the perpetrator is supposed to have been someone who gives love and provides care. Feelings of unworthiness usually develop. After all, why would something so disgusting happen unless "I deserved it." People have to work through those feelings and then try to forgive the person who abused them. **It is tough work and truly represents what we mean by "working through" an issue.**

An example of a regression follows in which far-reaching implications emerge in the present life. One of the effects in the present life of the incest in the previous life is abnormally severe pain at the menses.

(We're looking for a past-life cause for severe pain at the menses.) There's ivy and low bushes, below knee-level. There's a log cabin, a door, and windows with openings. There's a table and some kind of fowl. I get the sense of a very big man. I'm a woman. I feel like a child—about twelve or thirteen. I'm serving his dinner.

(Later.) I see my stuffed animals on my bed. I'm going to go to bed. I have some anxiety. I'm stuck. (Showed a lot of anxiety, but wouldn't go to the cause.)

(Later.) I feel like I'm grown up now. I feel like I'm in the same house, but he's gone.

(Did he die?) Yes.

[We now try to back into the trauma because it's obviously too painful for her to experience as the child. As the adult looking back over what happened, she can discuss it. Because of her obvious anxiety around going to bed, it was pretty clear what was happening to her. That's why I knew what question to ask.]

(Did he molest you?) Yes. That's why I'm alone—alone in the house. I don't want to have anything to do with anybody.

(How did he die?) I feel responsible. I think I did it. A knife. I see a knife. I think I stuck it into him.

(Was he coming after you again?) Yes. I went to tell the authorities. It's out in the open. They must have let me off. God, he was so heavy. I couldn't breathe.

(Preceding death.) I'm old. I'm on that same bed. My hair's gray. I just feel so old. I don't feel anything. I never let anybody know.

(Was he your father?) Yes.

(Following the death.) I see the body. I really feel like

*I'm floating. I don't feel afraid. **I feel I should have trusted myself—trusted myself that I was okay, that there
wasn't anything wrong with me. It wasn't my fault.
I felt like I was filthy dirty and couldn't be with a
nice man.** He said that and I believed him.*

(What was the lesson?) **Trust myself.**

*(Move to that higher level of consciousness, to what we
call the High Self.)*

(Is the pain from that lifetime?) I believe so.

(What needs to be released?) Guilt. Responsible.

(Are you able to see that you are not responsible?) Yes.

(Are you able to let go?) Don't know.

*(Is there physical trauma?) Yes. [Worked on cleaning
out the sense of filth she described and healing the body.]*

*(Is there emotional trauma?) Trust. Self-acceptance.
Purge. Fear of something, of letting go. Guilt and responsibility. Get word "control."* **Letting go of control is
the fear.** *If lets go might not be safe. The child did not
have control.*

*(Is the drive to eat food another way of being safe?)
Correct. The choices were repeated. The lesson apparently
unlearned. [The client also had an eating disorder and that
is why the question was asked. Some believe that those
who have been sexually molested may put on weight as a
protection around the body]*

Alive Again...Again...and Again

(Is there mental trauma?) Unworthiness.

(Can that be released at this time?) Yes. (Good.)

(Is there trauma at the spiritual level?) Uniqueness.
Why left alone? She was forgotten. Not connected.

*(Her present pain?) She will not allow the memory. I
hear screaming. The body remembers.*

(Could it affect any present relationships?) It has.

(Is there a message from the High Self?) **I'd like to
tell her to trust herself, to free herself, and that she
is loved.**

LEARN FROM YOUR PAIN

So, we have seen many ways that individuals are blocked
from perceiving their power. These traumas or wounds to
the soul interfere with the individual's clear perception and
acceptance of the self. **When the causes are acknowledged,
the power can be regained.** Perhaps you have had feelings
similar to some of the people whose stories you have read.
Maybe reading their stories will help you let go of any
wound to your soul and reclaim your power. **Learn what
you can from your pain and then try to let it go.
Forgiveness for the person who injured you is a helpful
step if you are to truly "let it go" and free yourself to enjoy
the power that is your rightful heritage.**

Chapter VI

Marriage and Family

*M*arriage is probably the most difficult relationship in which to find success. With a child, one more easily forges a bond that will last a lifetime. Marriage to another unrelated adult, as often as not, develops into a relationship of hate and resentment. Gina Cerminara, author of **Many Mansions (Penguin USA)** and other excellent books on reincarnation, attributed a quotation to Shakespeare during one of her lectures. I have been unable to find the source. However, it is related to our discussion, though in a humorous way. It goes like this:

> *If someone is wrecking your life,*
> *Don't reach for a gun or a knife.*
> *Better love them today,*
> *Or brother, you may*
> *Come back as a husband and wife.*

Marriage seems to be a crucible for the working out of issues in relationships and settling of karma. It seems that

those souls with whom you incarnate in the family are those with whom you have already had associations and issues on which you are mutually working.

What constitutes a good or successful marriage? If we consider the earlier discussions of why a soul would choose to incarnate—to learn lessons—we could assume that any marriage is good because lessons are being learned. Trying to avoid the use of "good" and "bad" in regard to life experiences is difficult. Words I try not to use in my classes and with clients are "good," "bad" and "should." If we ask what constitutes a successful marriage, and **define successful as a relationship in which all members of the relationship feel nurtured, loved, and supported and have attained a feeling of peace or serenity with one another, then we can look at those lifetimes in which those characteristics are present and say they are successful.** Marriage is not appropriate for everyone. Having children is not appropriate for everyone. Sometimes marriage and children are not consistent with your life purpose. But how many young adults would consider doing an inventory of their life, determining what their life purpose is, and proceeding accordingly? Most of us do not know our life's purpose until it is time to leave and that is a little late.

MARRIAGE TAKES WORK

Mandatory counseling before any marriage would help. It is unlikely that that will ever occur and, anyway, it would be a violation of individual rights. Consider the learning that could take place before the marriage so that a more painful process of learning would not have to occur during and after the marriage. Would it not be wiser to discover before marriage that your intended mate includes infidelity in his or her options than to discover later that you both do not share the same views on this activity? Would it not be wiser to discover that your intended has an addiction to alcohol or some other activity or substance and is verbally or physically abusive before the marriage? Of course, even if intended mates do not appear to manifest these characteristics, people change and these traits could still manifest.

COMMITMENT IS IMPORTANT

Work, work, work is what is required for a successful marriage. Rarely, if ever, has there been a marriage or long-term relationship when one or both of the partners have not felt disenchanted or disconnected. **That is why commitment is so important. If there is a low level of commitment, there will not be much energy available to work through those "down" times.** One has to believe that the advantages of a marriage or long-term commitment are worth the investment. Today, many do not believe that a marriage is worth that kind of commitment. And . . . maybe in many cases it is not. The marriage would need to be the most important relationship in your life, next to your relationship to yourself—yes, even more important than your relationship to your children. It is useful to look at what seem to be necessary elements for a successful marriage and what are elements that will surely destroy a marriage. That is why work is required. As we have said in earlier chapters, these are times for accelerated growth. If one partner wants to work on the relationship and the other chooses not to participate, then sometimes the one who wants to grow must leave the relationship. However, unless there is physical danger, that action should not be taken without much thought and introspection.

Couples are together for a reason and lessons are to be learned from one another. **To leave a relationship without learning as much as one can from it would be leaving oneself open for another opportunity to learn those lessons.**

COMMUNICATION AND INDIFFERENCE

Communication is necessary for a successful relationship. Of the regressions I have observed over the years, many of the most painful were those where little or no communication occurred between the partners, and one partner felt isolated. Sometimes the lack of communication occurs because one partner does not know how to communicate, but often it is the result of indifference. **Indifference is one of the most deadly and destructive aspects of a relationship.** While some partners are withering from the lack of connection or nurturing, the other partners go about their business oblivious of the pain they have caused and, probably, basically unaware that they have not contributed to the relationship. **There seems to be a perception over the centuries that providing a home and food for your mate and children is sufficient contribution to the marriage and little is done to support the bond between the couple. One does that much for farm or zoo animals; that is not a marriage.**

Let us look at a couple of regressions in which there was indifference by one of the partners. The first example is an extreme one in that it shows how resentment from indifference can fester into hatred which, in our first example, became murderous. Think about yourself. **Which is more painful, to have someone engage you in arguments and disagreements, or to have someone be indifferent to your needs or your concerns?** Quite frankly, to have a marriage partner be indifferent to whether you are there or not is probably one of the most painful realizations for those trying to understand why they are so unhappy in their marriage. It hurts deeply. And, in the example that follows, it hurt deeply enough to want revenge.

(Where are you?) I'm in a city and there are houses on each side of the road. It's cobblestone. I'm male and I have on tights with balloon pants. The houses appear to be half-timbered and kind of overhanging. But, this is a very wide street.

(Go to the place where you live.) I'm seeing a house by a river and it's a big house. This man has a short, kind of pointed beard and blonde/brown hair and a narrow face. This house is also timber and stucco, but it's straight up and down—not overhanging. It has a big garden around it. There are lots of grass and trees, shrubs and greenery. Inside there is a lot of wood paneling and a big fireplace. There are highly carved chairs padded in velvet. It's a rich room. The candlesticks are silver. There's a big chest along the wall and a big carved table. The windows in this room are basically colored glass.

*There's a woman in this room who is very richly dressed. She's in a velvet gown with the ruffle around the neck. She has a cap on the head like a Dutch cap. These people are middle-aged. They don't fight, but I think they're just married. There doesn't seem to be any emotions involved. There's almost an **indifference,** but he doesn't dislike her. Just indifferent.*

(Later.) There are two teenaged boys. The wife is trying to manipulate the boys to do something. I sense a fight for

control. She's trying to turn these boys against their father, but it's very subtle. He's beginning to realize she's doing this. He has been indifferent. He's more interested in what he does. He's a minister to a king or something. He's close to a power seat. I think this is a man who has tunnel vision and is not truly aware of the people around him. He is also a man who keeps his feelings bottled up.

He lives in a time where most of the men are very lecherous and he's not. He's very much on the straight and narrow. The problem is, he's indifferent to her (the wife). I think what he's done to her. . . he's kept her at home. He goes off and she stays at home.

(Later.) He's in some kind of a council meeting. They're debating whether or not to go to war. I'm seeing him march off to war with this huge army. Very opulent tents. They're not "roughing it." They are also very close to a walled city. It's on some kind of mountain and this army is in a valley. Lots of pennants flying. I'm English and we're at war with France. [The client slips into the person at this time. She has been observing.] We're on French soil. We're milling around. They just appear to be camped. I think they've actually captured this city. The king is there. He's a large man and he's very dark. I appear to be being shoved out of center stage and appear to be in the perimeter of power at this stage. I get the feeling this man (back to the observer) is very much opposed to being there, but because of loyalty and fear of losing his power base, he's there. His eyes are too close together. Feel like he'd almost rather be a monk, but he's a Protestant. He wants power on the one hand, but won't do just anything to gain control. Also, I don't think he has the brains for it. Not dumb, though. He doesn't have the charisma and the brains to be a great leader. He's wise enough to be heard in council, but not lead. He appears to be able to only focus on one thing at a time.

(Later.) He's back in his home and the boys are grown. He's suddenly realized that the boys are trying to take over. They want some of his power and their inheritance early. He's shocked that they don't like him—why they're **indifferent** to him? The wife and two boys are making demands for something. He's shocked at being attacked by them. The oldest son wants some kind of power that the father could give him and he's fighting it. The younger son supports it. The wife is presenting the case in a cold logical manner with tremendous anger under it. Whatever it is, he's going to give in.

(Later.) He's riding away from the house. He's given in to their demands and he's going off to live by himself someplace. It's like he's an old beaten man. He goes to some kind of castle. I'm not even sure it's in the same country. He's older and the sons are middle-aged. There's countryside.

(Preceding death.) He's sitting at a table with a lot of books on it. It looks like he has a heart attack. He's all alone in this room. I'm not sure if he's had a heart attack or was poisoned. He was drinking and then had this seizure. He was not real old, but acts like an old beaten man. He's just surprised he's dead. Feel like he moved to Spain or Portugal and lived in this castle-like place. I think his sons had him killed. He was so indifferent to them. They did it to get their inheritance.

He was not a bad man, just indifferent to this family. He did what was expected.

Alive Again...Again...and Again

(What was the lesson he came to learn?) Not to be so self-absorbed. Don't think he learned it. Maybe that's my perception. This man thought he was being kind and was absolutely astounded when he found out people didn't perceive his actions as kind. This man really would have been a monk except that he lived in a Protestant society. The disciplines of a monk are more to his taste. He really doesn't feel great sorrow when he rides away from the family. It was a huge relief that he could walk away. **He had just married and had children because it was expected.**

(Move to that higher level of consciousness we call the High Self.) He made his judgments and was very stiff with them. **He was a man with no love in him.**

This was a man who, by society's standards, did all the **right things. But, there was no love, no feeling, no passion for his family. They were never first with him. What probably began as hurt, likely became anger and resentment and then grew into hatred.**

WORK BEFORE FAMILY

Another successful businessman put most of his energy into his work instead of his family. When he was older he had a sense of, **"Is that all there is?"** His story follows.

(Where are you?) I might be in a building. There are envelopes underneath my arm. I have on a white shirt and black pants, and am walking down a corridor. It's a big place with a lot of doors. The building is all white. Seems like I'm going to a room. The room's already open. There's a wood desk and a plain chair and a light on the table. It

seems like I'm working on some papers or something.

*(Later.) I'm getting something that looks like a church. Seems like it has a white picket fence around it. It has a lot of stones in it. It's a wood entryway and real nice paneling. There's several rooms—library, den, dining room, etc. It's more than one story. There's a large stairway that is all wood. Seems like there's a lot of kids around, but **I can't be bothered with them.** I go into the library to work and read. There's a fire going. Lots of books. I sit in this easy chair and someone brings me this drink on a tray. I'm content. I'm older, 40's, gray at the temple, still have black curly hair. I have one of those watches on a chain. It seems **I know there's a family outside that room, but I don't want to go deal with them or talk to them.** I smoke my pipe.*

(Later.) Now I get a sense there might have been a fire and we rebuilt part of the house. I also sense that maybe my wife died in the fire, but the kids are still there. It didn't burn the whole house down, just part of it. It started in the kitchen. I see great big flames. I'm standing outside and I'm watching the fire. I think we have several kids and we must have nannies or someone taking care of them now.

(Go back to the time before the fire.) I'm at an office and it seems like I'm working real hard. There's other men, maybe bosses. They're standing over me while I'm working. Seems to have an accountant's visor on and sleeves rolled up. It seems like they're getting excited over something I'm working on. It's like we discovered something. Whatever it is, they're real happy about it. Seems like I'm pretty young. We're running around with little papers in our hand. Don't know if just made a lot of money or know how.

Alive Again...Again...and Again

I flashed to a house. It wasn't anything like the later house. I see a wife holding a baby. She's a big, robust woman with an apron on and hair up. It doesn't seem like we have a whole lot to talk about when I come home. I'm real attached to the baby. I'm playing with the baby. It seems pretty boring.

(Later.) I get the feeling the baby was a boy and he went into business with me. I'm really proud of him. He's going to take it over. I guess we were happy. I worked a lot and made a lot of money, but sense, "Is that all there is?" I think I really missed her (the wife). I don't know what I'd do without my work (an addiction?) and that's why I'm always working.

(Where was this?) I sense Chicago (this client has never been to Chicago). The business building was whitish. In the back of the house were a lot of trees and a lake.

(Is there a college there?) I can see me on campus. Big campus. Long way between buildings. (Northwestern?) That feels right. I have a warm feeling for the school.

(Go to the fraternity house.) It's a two-story building. Not fancy. There's two to a room. Messy. Clothes everywhere. Beta (I named several fraternities?) feels more right. Harry or Henry. I think it's Harry. For some reason I get Galvin (for the last name).

(Go to time preceding death.) I seem fairly old, 50's, maybe late 50's. I'm in that den sitting in that chair with all the books—seems that was my favorite place. I'm slouched over in that chair. It doesn't seem like I was sick, just gave up. It was time to go. It seems like I was moving

slower before that time, maybe from loneliness, too. I don't think any of the kids live in the house anymore. I still have the servants. I'm wearing a lovely maroon jacket and ascot. Seemed like I had a lot of money and people seemed to like me. It doesn't seem like I had any enemies. The servants were sorry to see me go because I treated them well. I died in 1952.

(Move to that higher level of consciousness, to what we call the High Self.)

(Are any of those business skills present in this lifetime?) Yes. Organization came up first. Determination. Seems like working lots. Do something on her own. Want to say, start a small business. It's going to be artsy. Maybe crafts. Seems like I'm going to make things with my hands. And . . . get a sense of things made out of wood that I've painted. There's dried flowers—that kind of thing. More like a boutique. I see photography on the walls, too. It may have something to do with paintings. I see myself managing it and working there sometimes, and other times out trying to find things for the store. I know what people want so I'll be out trying to buy things that will sell. It will be things I would want myself and don't want to leave in the store, but would want to take home.

This person is career-oriented and was working on determining her skills and strengths and where she might direct her energies in the future. She is not married and does not foresee wanting children. She was born after the death of the gentleman above and has never been to Chicago. I had a sense she worked in the Wrigley building and lived in Evanston on Lake Michigan. She did not know there were homes along the lake. **In this lifetime she has avoided** longterm relationships, and, though she loves to work her-self, has avoided dating any workaholic, successful types.

ACCEPTANCE

In another regression which will follow, what began as an indifferent, dispassionate relationship developed into a close and rewarding experience. **Acceptance is the important emotion in this story. A nonpassionate relationship developed into one of deep caring.**

> *(You are on a path. Describe the vegetation.) I see pink roses—wild roses along a fence. I'm sensing a farm house with modest wooden furniture, wooden rocking chair and round wooden table. My wife is setting the table. She has long brown hair and has a hat on. The hat is sort of in her hair. We're having roast or mutton. I'm male. There's a little girl with brown curly hair. We're close, but not like the last time, though. (He's referring to another regression in which he was very close with his family.)*
>
> *(Later.) Somebody's in bed and sick. I don't think it's me. It's my little girl. She's sleeping. I'm not very responsive, I feel a little distant. The wife is in the kitchen. Wasn't the warm feeling I had before.*
>
> *(Go to the time of your wedding.) We're kneeling at an altar. Here she has curly hair and is young, like sixteen or seventeen. She's attractive. I don't sense strongly attached to each other. I'm sort of neutral. I don't object, but also no strong attraction.*
> *(Go back to when you made the decision to marry.) Now her hair isn't as curly. She's more attractive. We're*

out in the country by a stream. We're more intimate. There is an attraction. She's cute. We're not passionate, we're friends. I'm not proposing to her at that point. I feel the decision was made for us. I'm not proposing to her.

(Were women given to men?) Yes. That's the feeling.

(Later.) It's a party. My daughter's having a birthday party. It's inside the house. She has girlfriends sitting around the table. She's happy and about seven or eight years old. She's happy, she has her friends—it's good.

(Later.) I'm looking at an old metal mailbox on the fence. It's like I'm waiting for mail—waiting to hear from somebody. I'm just sitting there waiting. It's a letter. It has some seals on it. It's an official letter of some sort. There's a seal on the upper left-hand corner of the letter. It's either going into the army or foreclosure. My first thought was conscription. The seal sort of turned into the head of a horse.

(Later.) I'm on a stagecoach. I think I'm reporting somewhere. I do place it around the Civil War. It's a blue uniform, more of a light than a dark, maybe it's gray. I think I'm a Confederate.

(Later.) I'm right by a cannon. Now I'm on a hill. I've really got mixed emotions about being in that war. I don't have a passion for fighting in that war. I was pulled into it just like I didn't want to open that letter. The seal was a horse pulling a piece of artillery. What's going through my mind is how to extricate myself from this situation. That was an emotional war and I'm not emotionally involved. I'm from Tennessee. We had no colored servants where I

Alive Again...Again...and Again

come from. I respected my family. I don't think I was into marriage and I don't feel torn from there or longing to be back, but don't like being in this war either.

(Later.) Now I'm on a mountain near a cannon over-looking a river. I sense a big battle. I'm not afraid. I'm detached. I'm not afraid to die and I'm not in a state of panic. I'm part of the artillery. People are trying to come up that mountain. We have the advantage. I don't feel life-threatened.

Oops, I just got shot in the leg. It's the right leg across the knee. There's just a sharp twinge. I think the bullet went through it. I'm on the ground. There's not much I can do. I'm out of it. I can't put weight on it. I'm sitting under a tree thinking about my predicament. I'm by myself. There's bodies around and I'm all by myself. The cannons aren't active—no one is firing them. I survive the battle. Those who were alive went somewhere else. I see people on the opposite side of the hill and they're retreating. I think it's our group.

I see a Union soldier now. I think I'm being taken captive. They're helping me with my leg and putting a splint on it. I'm being treated okay. I don't have strong feelings against the Union. I'm just not involved in this war.

(Later.) I have the feeling I'm in a barracks or detention area, a prisoner of war camp. It's sort of a flat area. Not Tennessee. Not a lot of growth. A plain of some sort. I think I was taken northwest to Ohio. I'm just sitting out the war.

(Later.) I'm just on a buckboard. I think I'm going home. I'm riding in an open buckboard, coming to the

home. It's sort of pretty. It's autumn. I see my wife and we hug. My daughter's about fourteen or fifteen. It's nice to be home. They're happy to see me. It's modest. We're not a people of means. My wife took care of the whole thing. The daughter looks good. The farm looks fine. I think it's tobacco. I get the feeling it was very adequate—gave us what we needed. The lifestyle was pretty good.

(Preceding death.) I'm in a chair, a big wicker chair. I'm dressed in coveralls or whatever. I just think I had a heart attack in that chair. I'm in my seventies with white hair which is receding. I'm bald in front with curly bushy hair in back. My wife and daughter are both there. There is sorrow. **I feel that the relationship grew closer and closer over time, after the war. I feel closer to them now.**

(What was the lesson?) **Acceptance comes to mind.** *Wasn't much I could do about pre-arranged wedding. I could accept or not accept. The wife was a good person. I wasn't romantically enthralled with her, but I decided to make the best of it. I didn't have my heart in the war, but I wasn't going to desert. I didn't mind being captured—it was probably where I'd rather have been. I wasn't chicken, I just wasn't where I wanted to be.*

The acceptance left open the possibility for the relationship to take a turn. If I was in a state of resistance, it couldn't have happened. It was a reason for me to survive the war.

This man was in a dispassionate relationship and, at the time of this regression, he was exploring the possibilities of any future for it. There were many positive aspects of the relationship such as communication, respect and great

friendship. He stayed and decided to allow it to take its natural course.

LOOKING FOR JOY

A woman who had a very unpleasant childhood and a
not particularly happy adulthood was looking for a joyful
time to give her some reference point for joy. In the following
regression, she,too, had an arranged marriage and there is
acceptance of things she couldn't change; but there is also the
element of joy throughout most of the lifetime.

> *(Where are you?) I see sand, I'm barefooted. It's a
> hutch, thatched with poles. We eat as a family and cooking
> is done in the thatch with the small hole in top. The main
> meal, I guess, is the evening meal. It looks like a yellow
> mushed substance. There's been a hunting party so we're
> having meat. I'm female, about four or five years old.
> There's a mother and father and I have quite a lot of broth-
> ers and sisters. The boys outnumber the girls. Mother's
> very loving—she has time for all of us. In this particular
> culture that's her job—thatch, preparation of meals and
> children. She has kind eyes, soft eyes. Father, oh, he's very
> proud of his offspring. He is extremely proud that he has
> three sons. Girls are okay, but more boy babies means more
> hunting and more things for the group. I don't get the feel-
> ing of very much joy. (She was already getting the message
> that boys were more desirable than girls.)*

> *(Go to a significant event.) We're going for pearls, div-
> ing for pearls. The girls are good at it. It's fun splashing in
> the water and seeing the fish. Things have been put down
> at certain depths and we have to go down and pick up*

things and bring them up. We do a lot of this. The mothers seem to be getting a big kick out of this. The teenage girls are teaching us. I feel more like a polywog. The women are weaving nets. I think this is fun. You can see the pretty fish and the coral.

(Another significant event?) I'm older and now I know what we're supposed to do (regarding the diving). Some areas are better than others. If an area is depleted, then we go to another area. I have things on a belt in which we put the things we find. When it's full, we dump it out.

(Later.) My sister is getting married. She is the eldest. There are all sorts of "rigamarole" that must be done. She doesn't even get to pick the husband. I wonder about me. Will I marry a total stranger or my best friend? There's a big feast and she has a circle of something on her head that she has to make. She has to go into the woods to find this special bush. It's all very mysterious. She puts something on her ankles. She wears a skirt of some sort—like a grass skirt. She's barefooted.

(Later.) Oh, my mother's had another baby—a cute little guy. It's another little round baby boy. I love him. I sort of take over with him. My parents don't seem to mind. I sing to him. I'm very happy with him.

(Later.) My parents think it's my time to get married and I'm frightened. I only want to marry one person. We've snuck off and talked about it. It has to be decided by the elders. Oh, no, it's not my friend. Because I'm so good with children, they decide I should marry a man who already has a family. I cry myself to sleep. My parents go to the elders and persuade them to let me marry my friend. **My joy**

Alive Again...Again...and Again

knows no bounds. I can't believe it. I hug my parents. The elders decide that another girl who is older can marry the other man. I don't care if I have to dive all day.

(Go to time of your wedding.) I wanted to do things differently. I go off into the woods to make a hairpiece. I want flowers. I find a plant that has the most fragrant flower. I weave that in. My female friends go crazy about it. I also put flowers in my anklet. I get flowers for my mother—for her hair. I get lots of flowers and put them on food platters. This is fun.

The elders get together and everyone comes out. It takes all day to get hitched. There's food and dancing. The flowers look nice. My friend is grinning from ear to ear. He's done what the men have to do—he's built a hut which is away from all the other huts. At first I thought that was scary. I go to inspect it. He put flowers in a wooden bowl.

I'll still have to do things for my family and his. That's just the way it is. I don't feel put upon. I have to start making some utensils.

(Later.) There's a lot of confusion where we live. Oh, I think there's another tribe and they're going to be attacking our camp. We've made preparations as best as possible. We all get everybody as close together as possible. We get down close to the water—don't want anyone to get in back of us. Everyone is pulling together. It's the first time I've been part of these preparations. Shields are all planted into the ground to form a barrier. I didn't want

Alive Again...Again...and Again

to leave our hut, but that's the best way to go right now.

(Later.) Oh, I've had a baby—a little baby girl. I guess times have changed. My husband adores her. It's not the feeling I had when I was growing up that women were less than they should be. He's just amazed that we've created a human being.

(Go to time preceding death.) I'm in another hut. Oh, it's the hut one of the elders had when I was a little girl. I guess that makes my husband an elder. I can't walk very well. All my children are married and have children. I'm old. My husband is still living. He has a cane and is all bent-over. We've lived a long time. We've seen lots of changes.

(Do you see the body?) I see the body.

(What was was the lesson you came to learn?) **To have fun. It was a happy, joyful life. Get togethers were always happy occasions.**

Joy and happiness in a relationship over a lifetime were achieved in the above regression. The couple, the society was able to have fun. What would that be like in our culture today? Is it attainable? Is it worth striving to achieve? Obviously we cannot duplicate that culture, but are there lessons to be learned from such a simple existence? To run off to an island to try to create that kind of a peaceful existence could be an option, but doing so would not offer the learning opportunities of staying in this culture and incorporating some of the elements of that kind of life in your life today.

Alive Again...Again...and Again

A Nurturing Society

An entire social system that supports the nurturing of the individual is what is seen in the next regression. Again, it is not a lifestyle that is easily available in our culture nor one that would necessarily be desired. However, some elements of that lifestyle might be desirable to many. The client was very happy in that lifetime. Today her life is very different. In the life you are about to see, she stayed in the same house and the same village most of her life and felt comfortable and supported. In her present life, her husband likes to move and they have both a winter home and a summer home. These moves have been very stressful for her. Just when she finally adjusts to the move, makes her nest and establishes friends and activities, it is time to go to the other home and the process begins all over again. In the regression, we were looking for insight into why these moves have been so difficult for her. Her story follows. It is a story that left me wondering. It is what I call a **"warm and fuzzy"** life.

(Describe the vegetation along the path.) The grass is high, almost knee-high. I have on red shoes and they're flat with a little strap across with a button. My legs are bare. The path is narrow and it is dirt. It's like a meadow. I see a building in the distance like a farmhouse with a turret or silo next to it. Other people are working in the fields nearby and they're wearing peasant clothing. As we get closer, we smell the food and I'm hungry. They're good smells. I walk in and there's a big woman there and she is cooking some things in the fireplace. She's loving me and saying she's so glad I came. She calls two other children and says, "Look who's here," and we hug and kiss. She wanted me to see a new calf who was born. A man is milking and he's happy to see me. These are relatives. We go back inside

and bow our heads and say a prayer. We're all laughing and eating. I think I must go back home, but they say to stay the night. I stay on a straw mattress and cover with rough muslin.

(Later.) There's like narrow cobblestone streets with people around leading donkeys. Everyone's greeting everyone else. Women have on big flowing skirts. They are pounding clothes by the bank. There's lots of noise and commotion. There's a dark hut near others with openings for windows. The openings are covered with oilskin. The building is made of stone and bricks together. It's dark. I want to be back in the country. Too much commotion and noise. Too crowded. I can walk to the relatives.

Inside there's a table—kind of rickety, an earth floor, straw in the corner and, in front of the fireplace, a black thing for pots.

(Later.) There's bells ringing. People have packs on their backs and are all bent over. A man comes, drops his pack and says he's so tired. He says he's sad because something happened to the family. He's sad because he's worried. Something happened to my mother and she's sick and someone's taking care of her. She's in a bed and a couple of women are around. She looks drawn and doesn't look like she's going to get well. Someone's supposed to get herbs. I want to go back to the country.

(Later.) I'm in another city somewhere and it's bigger. I'm older and dressed differently. I came through a big gate and am walking down the street. It's some kind of a holiday and fair. I'm dressed in clothes I like. People are saying hello. I'm excited to be there. There's a lot of gaiety. I'm

about seventeen, my name is Marisha and it's in Czechoslovakia. I'm working there, but not today because it's a holiday. People are dancing in a circle and someone's playing a flute. People have come in from the villages. I'm living with a different family now, but they're good to me. I think I'm helping them on the farm. They're good loving people. They have a daughter who helps also. Father married someone else.

*(Later.) I'm in my own place. It's like a little cottage. It's in the country. I'm married and I have a child. **I'm very happy with the husband and so happy to be there.** I'm singing to the baby girl and my husband comes in between chores to hug me and the child. I made clothes for the child. My friend on the other farm also comes to see me. My friend is not married. I'm about twenty-three and my husband is John.*

*(Later.) We're living in the same cottage and we have four children, two boys and two girls. I'm teaching them things. They're playing and laughing. My friend comes over and now she has two children. There are a lot of animals around. We seem to have prospered. **It's a very happy and fulfilling life. I'm very contented and think how nice life is, how good it is.***

(Later.) My daughter's getting married and everyone's gathered around. She's going far away and I know I won't see her enough. I'm sad and I'm happy. I like the man. Everyone's brought food. She's so happy. There are ribbons in her hair. He says he'll take good care of her. His family is there. We all like one another. It's a happy time. My husband has gotten heavier. He looks different but has some warm shining eyes. I hope my daughter's marriage is the same way.

Alive Again...Again...and Again

(Later.) I'm very upset and sad. My son's been injured and hurt. There's blood all over him. His leg is mangled and we can't save it. It takes a long time to heal but we're together all the time. He has crutches and he learns to walk. He's strong and he manages. He's about eighteen or nineteen.

(Later.) I'm a lot older. My hair is gray. I've gotten fat. I don't get around as quickly as I used to. My husband has died. The children come. I still have my old friend. She comes and we hug and kiss. The grandchildren come. A neighbor helps with the animals. I don't go out as much. When I go, I know the people in the village. I'm still very content. **I liked the farm and being in one place all my life. I knew the people and they were hardworking, caring people.**

(Preceding death.) I'm in this bed and my children are all around and they're whispering. They're concerned and they're crying, and I tell them not to worry. I've had a good life. My friend is there holding my hand. I'm ready to go. I'm sixty-two.

(After death.) Sort of like it's beautiful colors—lovely and peaceful. **I see my children crying and I'm so happy. I wish I could tell them I'm very happy.** *My husband is waiting and he's so happy, and he tells me he's been waiting for me. It's nice.*

(What was the lesson you came to learn?) **I came to experience love, caring, and friendship—that you can be very content just having people you love around you. Stay strong and it will be okay. It's easy to be happy, if you don't try to take in too much or do too much. It's simple, if people love you.**

Alive Again...Again...and Again

What a beautiful lifetime! It might be boring by some standards, but, again, it offers insight into what elements bring happiness to an individual. **Being connected to and loved by other individuals seems to be worth more than wealth.**

RESPECT AND CRITICISM

Respect seems to be a necessary component of marriage. Each person needs to feel valued. Criticism is another killer of a relationship. When one constantly criticizes another, one is giving the message that you are not okay—that something is wrong with you. **Those who criticize the most are usually the ones who are most unhappy with themselves.** An interesting dynamic of the personality is that **we project on others what we fear most in ourselves.** We criticize most in others what we fear most in ourselves. Look at yourself. Are you critical of those around you? Do you feel comfortable with who you are? A person comfortable with herself is not threatened by others or how others do things.

Thanksgiving dinner for many families is a good example of where lack of respect or criticism is often experienced. How many times have you heard stories of couples fighting because of statements like those which follow? "My family always has at least two kinds of dressing for dinner and mashed potatoes and mincemeat pie"? Or, "I don't like mincemeat pie and my family has always had sweet potatoes and broccoli." If it is too threatening to let go of old ways of doing something in order to create a new tradition, then one way of doing something has to be right and one way has to be wrong. **There can be no respect if there can only be a right and a wrong way of doing something.** If one perceives that both ways of doing something have value, then there is no threat—one merely decides how one wants to do something at any given time.

Arguments often occur when one partner perceives that the other partner does not have respect for the other or respect for the feelings and thoughts of the other. Arguments also occur when one partner does not respect the other and does not want to be bothered with the feelings and ideas of the other. Respect is the accepted way you treat business associates and others outside the home. Should you not expect the same treatment from your mate as a friend or business associate would receive?

In the following regression the couple seemed to have much respect for one another.

> *(Describe the vegetation along the path.) There are flowers, grass, fir trees and mountains. The dwelling is like a half-timber Bavarian house. It's pretty light inside. There's furniture inside. There's a pot of stew with potatoes and vegetables. There's a table and other people are there. We're not yet sitting. We're just putting the food on the table. I'm female, between teenage and young adult. Mother and father are there and younger children. I'm the oldest. In fact, I'm a lot older than the rest of the children.*

> *(Later.) It's snowing. I'm about the same age. Outside there's a horse-drawn carriage. It's a sleigh with runners on it. I think it's Christmas time. We're going down the hill. I think we're just outside of town and we're going to go into town. There's like a party or a dance. Father is driving the carriage. Everybody is laughing and smiling—it's exciting. We're easy people, happy people.*

*(Have you arrived. yet?) I'm there. It's like a commu-
nity center or hall. There's tables lined up on the outside.
There's punch and food. People are already dancing in cir-
cles—not individually. There's someone special. He's sort
of a husky man. He is wearing knee-length liederhosen. He
has a very chubby face and is real warm. His eyes are
bright and I feel really warm in my chest. Right now we
just sort of stand there giggling. He keeps smiling. He's tall
and big. I'm somewhat shorter. I have on a scarf and braids.
We dance. It's a circle dance. After the dance is over, he just
says good-bye to me and we go home. He stops my father
and says something to him. I know that he's asking him if
he can marry me.*

*(Later.) It's like a May Day, I think. There's a pole. The
girls all have flowers and ribbons in their hair. Many are
blonde. Braids are tied up instead of down. There is definitely a German or Austrian feel to the clothing. There's a
meadow with fir trees on the outer part. I'm standing on
the sidelines just sort of watching. It's confusing. I know
I'm getting married soon, but I don't know if it's that day
or soon.*

*(Go to your wedding day.) We're in the same place, but
a different day. The pole is gone. Up the hill is the church.
The minister is there. He's like a priest, but not Catholic. I
keep feeling a sense of being somewhat fat. Everything feels
round on my body. But everyone is. I'm wearing light colors, but I feel a lot of embroidery is on my dress. Even
though it's springtime, it feels somewhat heavy. I keep getting a sense that these are very happy and carefree people.
It's not a big town and everyone is like family. **The whole
town is there. Anytime there's a wedding or anything, it's a major event for everyone.***

Alive Again...Again...and Again

*He's there. He keeps smiling. He has these
cheeks. All he does is smile. He's real quiet. We*
*couple of little Kewpie dolls. His eyes are very shiny and
bright. **I can feel the love.** He is so easy and comfortable
to be with. There are no feelings of apprehension at all. I
have a feeling he's a cheesemaker. That's where we live, too.
It's a cheese shop and the house is above it. In the back are
vats. It seems like it's a family thing. Someone else in the
family has goats and that's where we get milk. It's not like
we own the goats. Now I see that above the cheese house we
have a big room. The room is off to the side. It's a massive
room with a fireplace and woven rugs. I can tell that it's
half timber and the ceiling feels short. There's a railing that
goes down and some carvings. You can see the vats from up
there. It's warm and friendly and happy.*

*(Later.) There's a baby—mine—and it's fat, too. It
must be a girl. She has on a bonnet and a dress. We're in
the church. It's a baby christening. It's our second child.
The other is older now—maybe about three. It's a little boy.*

*(Later.) It's a funeral. It's my mother's. We have four
children. I see the stairs. We're happy. There just seems to
be a lot of warmth and happiness. No great events and no
tragedies. There was peace even with my mother leaving.
**There is an easiness about this life. Love and joy. And,
you just feel it.** (She's really enjoying the feelings at this
time and somewhat amazed.) Even with the children there's
just a sense of warmth. We do everything together. **We're
never angry. There's a lot of hugging and touching.**
You're just there. Each of the children is holding another's
hands. It's such a unit. I hug my husband a lot. We both
seem to be very quiet people. It's like we know each other.
We're very familiar with each other. We've known each*

Alive Again...Again...and Again

other all of our lives. We were never far apart from each other. When he comes in in the evening, he sits down and smokes his pipe. I'm busy in the kitchen, **but it's not far away. We're a part of each other. The kids are part of us, too.**

(Preceding death.) I'm in a window seat. It's the same house. The sun is coming down and it's real warm. There are a lot of quilts. Feel like I'm in my early sixties. He's still living. He still seems to be very strong and I just seem to be very tired. He's like a big bear.

(After death.) The body is in the same place. It's like I just felt very tired and went to sleep. My husband finds me. He's very calm about it. He just picks up the body and takes it somewhere. He knew it was going to happen. I think I've been sick a long time. He picked me up too easily.

(What was the lesson you had come to learn?) **Love. Even though hardworking, nothing seemed to be much of a hardship with love. Even with the townspeople, love was easily given and received. Even when it was cold, there was a sense of warmth. A lot of faith.**

This young woman had met a man for whom she had a strong attraction. She was looking for insight into why she was so attracted to him. We requested that she return to another lifetime when she had been with that soul. Whether she and that man ever get together probably is not as important as the experience of love she felt in that regression. She now has a different perception of what a marriage can be— one different from the commercials and movies. You might ask yourself if any of the elements of that period of time have any relevance to the world today? Maybe not, but I think so. Hopefully, warm and deeply loving feelings for another in a relationship will always have relevance.

COMMUNITY SUPPORT

Notice that in the last two lifetimes there was a lot of community support. Even when there was dancing, there was group dancing so everyone could be involved. Because, in our culture, couples and families are so isolated from one another, tremendous stress is put on the marriage. The couple has to be all things to each other. Not many individuals have the strength to manage that kind of responsibility. You would have to be very secure in your perception of yourself to be able to be nurturer, lover, companion, confidante, healer, workmate, business associate, parent, teacher, and other roles you might add.

Look at the role of business associate. Is not the average household like a business? In the past a family often was a business, working together to make cheese or manage a farm. **Today's family business is managing paper.** Have you ever compared the mail you now receive with that received a few years ago; or the number of bills you receive compared to the number your parents received when they were your age? How many checks do you write each month compared to ten years ago? In earlier generations, bills usually included a mortgage, gas and electric, water and telephone. Today you have many times more than that. You have to be a pretty astute business person just to understand the tax laws.

What family has just one car anymore? Perhaps a single person or a retired couple would have one car. In some cities,

such as New York and San Francisco, you can get along without a car but not in most places. Think about how much more
complicated your life becomes with each additional automobile. Each one requires insurance, license tags, smog checks
in some states, maintenance, fuel, parking and the list goes
on. One is always requiring maintenance.

LIFE IS COMPLICATED AND STRESSFUL

**Each additional task or chore complicates life more and
adds stress.** Many of us have been in the habit of saying that
there is no such thing as stress, it is just our reaction to certain events and it can be managed. I have learned that is not
necessarily so. We experience physical stress from noise;
from temperature changes such as moving out of a hot car
into a cold, air-conditioned building; from energy fields
around such things as electric blankets and appliances; from
some foods we eat and, probably, from many other sources
that we have yet to discover.

I was reminded of the truth of that recently when I was
using my daughter's waterbed in her old apartment while
working on this book. Over a year earlier, her baby had been
lying on the bed, which is heated, and my husband had felt
a current coming through the baby. He unplugged the bed
and the current stopped. The bed remained unplugged.
Before I came to use the apartment, new carpet was installed
and the bed had been disassembled and then reassembled by
a contractor. The first two nights I was there, I could not
sleep. I was edgy, almost to the point of feeling that my teeth
were on edge. Toward morning of the second night, I remembered that the bed had been reassembled and wondered if
the contractor had connected the plug. He had. I unplugged

it and could feel a difference right away. The edginess had been like an anxiety and it had stayed with me through part of the next day. After unplugging the bed, I had no more sleepless nights and no more anxiety.

How many insidious, unknown physical stressors such as that might any individual be experiencing? These stressors make it more difficult to deal with other stressors or stimuli. **When we are physically stressed, our reaction to other stimuli is more charged.** I can assure you that after a night on that electrical bed, I was jumpy the next day. I was not calm and serene. Add those known and unknown stressors to all the complications of living at this time, and the result is tremendous pressure on individuals and marriages. **Consequently, family members are out in the world each day being "stressed to the max," to borrow a popular phrase, and coming home, expecting to be nurtured, only to find everyone else is stressed. No wonder so few marriages survive.**

What I think we can learn from the regressions we have seen is that simplification can contribute to joy. Maybe we need to take an inventory of our lives, clearing away all that is unnecessary and removing as many stressors on the individuals and marriage as possible. **When the clutter is gone, perhaps the relationship will have a better chance.**

Finally, a regression follows which is one of my favorite love stories. Again, we were looking for a connection with another for whom the client felt deep love, her husband. In this past life they had very little in the way of material goods but they had a whole lot of love.

Alive Again...Again...and Again

(Where are you?) I see grass. There's a white house—a big white house. It's a mansion. It's light with furniture, a wood table. There's roast beef for dinner. There's a family with four children. I work there. I'm little, about four. I'm a little girl. Mommy works there. She prepares the food and I play. I play with the kids, but they have to eat. She's (the mother) black, she's kind of chubby. She has big eyes. They're sad. But she loves me. They're like almond eyes.

(Move to a significant event.) It's something with chickens, and guns, and being chased, and chickens running around. I'm older now, maybe thirteen. I'm frightened. I'm just staying out of the way. There are men getting hurt. The shooting has stopped. It's over.

(Later.) I'm in a shack. It's my own and I'm twenty-one. John is there (her husband in the present life) and we have one baby about a year old. We're happy together. We live in a little shack. John works. He works for someone else.

(Later.) It's something about downtown. We have the baby with us. We seem to be with the horses. We're in a wagon. It's not covered. I'm holding the baby. We went to the store and we're going to go home. We don't talk to the people. There are other black people, but they're not there now. We're not hated—just not liked. They don't bother us. I'm holding the baby pretty tight. Now we're back home. I don't look at anyone—I look away. I'm a loner. I don't bother them.
(Later.) There's trees all around the shack. I'm older. I have a boy. He and John are working in the field. There's an orchard with apple trees. We have just the boy.

(Later.) I'm sitting on the steps. I'm waiting. I have

Alive Again...Again...and Again

lemonade. It's getting dark. I keep seeing this car. I don't know why. There's a car. Not back yet. I'm a little worried. I don't know where they went. They're supposed to be home. They come home.

(Later.) John's older. We're both older. They were gone a long time. They went away. I was lonely. I was mellow, I didn't worry. I just missed them.

(Preceding death.) I'm still at the shack. I'm sitting in a chair. Old. John is already gone. Son doesn't live here. He's alright. I think I'm by myself. I'm just tired. I die in the chair.

(After the death.) I see the body. It has white hair and it's in the chair. The boy finds the body. He's crying. He's trying to hold me. He's just crying. He's glad I'm resting now, though.

(What was the lesson you had come to learn?) **It's about love. About loving. It was this kind of love that was calm and patient. Easygoing.** *Just minded our own business. It was love. It wasn't always safe, but it was comfortable with John and my boy. We didn't have very much at all. We wanted to, but we couldn't. In a way we didn't care. Felt lucky for the love. When John was away and came back, I remember him hugging me. There was this really secure feeling.*

A couple with very little in the way of material goods developed a deep love. In the regression above, the couple did not have the support of a strong community, in fact they were out there by themselves. Because of the kind of obstacles they faced and still maintained their love, this has been one of my favorite love stories.

Alive Again...Again...and Again

Hug Power

Notice that in the last few regressions, where there were successful marriage relationships, there was a lot of hugging. The people experiencing the regressions also fully experienced the hugs. Hugs must be powerful. Maybe we all need to be doing a lot more hugging. **I propose that another important element to a successful marriage is "hug power."**

Expectations of Marriage

What are the expectations of marriage? It seems that people who marry want the other person to take care of them and to make them happy. In the "old days,"expectations were that the woman would take care of her mate by preparing meals, cleaning the home, and taking care of any children. The male was expected to take care of the family by providing a home and food and the other niceties of life. Those expectations were fairly clear. How one person was supposed to make another person happy was never clear. Is "taking care" of the other partner supposed to create the happiness? One might assume so. If that is true, why were not the people in the first two regressions of this chapter happy? They certainly had more than adequate food and shelter. There must be more to this happiness thing than "taking care" of the other person.

Isolation

Ironically, one or both partners often isolate themselves from the other and then blame the other because they are not happy. We see this often with middle-aged men who have devoted their lives to a corporation or to their work and when they reach middle age, they are isolated from their wives and children and they are unhappy. This happens to women, too, and will, even more so, as they pursue business and professional careers. People think that they are unhappy because of their spouses, so they become involved with someone else, desperately hoping that that person can make them happy. And, for awhile, the excitement of a new relationship makes them feel that they are happier. In the meantime, **they have caused incredible, irreparable pain to their families and they still do not have a clue as to why they are so unhappy.**

COMMITMENT

There is tremendous pressure on the family today. That is why **there needs to be a commitment from both partners to work on the relationship, to study, and to understand the dynamics of problems as they arise. Study the problems in a relationship with the same kind of energy as you would problems that arise at work.** There must be a mutual "working through" of issues that arise. If that kind of attitude does not exist, then there is little hope for the survival of the marriage. Perhaps people should not marry and have a family until they feel that kind of commitment.

Recent research has shown that a strong marital bond was the one common factor in high-functioning happy families. That is not to say there cannot be happiness with single parents, for there can be. Strong bonds can be made with any kind of family. Since we have been working on marriage in this chapter, most of the references have been to marriages, but there has never been any intent to suggest that equally functional individuals cannot develop in families of

Alive Again...Again...and Again

another structure. Often the single-parent family is far superior to the conditions that were existing in the marriage, especially if violence or sexual abuse was involved. I am just saying that if there is a marriage, a strong marital bond supports development of healthy, happy children.

KNOW THYSELF AND THY MATE

"Know thyself" has been a motto I have stressed throughout this book. Now I will add, "Know thy Mate." The idea of an introspective, examined relationship is a Utopian idea, I realize. However, we must take marriage more seriously or not take it at all. **It can be an extremely powerful tool for growth, self esteem, happiness, serenity, and the development of well-balanced, healthy, happy children for future generations.** So what does that tell us happiness is? **Happiness seems to be feeling connected to self and other human beings in a loving, nonjudgmental way, and it is a feeling, a physical sensation.** I watched the clients as they were experiencing the regressions in which they were involved in deeply loving, caring relationships and they glowed. They could not get over how good it felt. They were happy. **Marriage is the crucible in which unconditional love is truly practiced. Neglect it and the pain is almost unbearable. Master it and the rewards are almost beyond imagination.**

Chapter VII

Celebration of Diversity

*R*ecognizing that all people love, struggle to make a life for themselves and their families, care for their children, bleed when they are cut, and mourn at the loss of loved ones reminds us that we are all human. Recognizing that we have more in common than not, reminds us that we are all human. Recognizing that we often take better care of our pets and our possessions than we do of other human beings reminds us that we have a long way to go before the recognition of our common humanity manifests into action.

Respect is the key—respect for those aspects of another that are different from our own. To celebrate the diversity of humankind—that would be the great adventure! You would not even have to be wealthy and travel the world; you could participate in the celebrations of the various cultures in your own community. How boring it would be if we were all the same.

Can you imagine a world without the lovely polynesian dances of Hawaii, or the elegant grace of the Asian woman in her native costume, or the vitality associated with the European Octoberfests, or the humor and energy unique to Black Americans, or the wonderful music that comes from so many different cultures? On and on and on. We are enriched by the diversity. **Why do we try to kill, or stamp out, or change that which enriches us most?**

Fools that we are, there is still hope. The face of war has changed. Or, shall we say, the "facelessness" of war has changed. Because of technological advances, we can now see the faces of the "enemy" as they grieve for their dead children, their dead sons and daughters in battle, their way of life. They bleed, they hurt, they cry—just like we do.

And how do we express our spirituality? How do we make sense of our place in the universe or universes? Many teachers have come to the planet to help us understand our relationship to one another and to a higher power. Universally, those teachers seem to say, we are to love one another as we would love ourselves. Or, they say, we are to treat others as we would want to be treated. Yet, we have spent thousands of years arguing over which teacher is "the" teacher of all teachers, and killing or banishing anyone who will not follow the "groupthink" or who dares to come to different conclusions from our own. Testaments to how little we have learned over the centuries are the millions and millions who have died or have been tortured because they were true to their own beliefs and could not accept the beliefs of the religion with the political power at any given time.

Alive Again...Again...and Again

Arrogance is a word that comes to mind to describe many religious leaders on the planet today and in earlier times. They take power that is not theirs to take and dare to tell others how they must live their lives. They have taken power from women and relegated them to a role of second class citizen. Because many of the words of these world teachers have been filtered through male-dominated cultures and have passed down through male writers, a bias exists toward males and against females. Physical strength and freedom from the chores of raising children and managing the home has allowed men to "take" the power they seek. In their arrogance, they have forgotten or perhaps they do not realize that they have forcibly taken that which does not belong to them—another's self-power.

What is "self-power"? It is the energy and freedom to manifest your own uniqueness as long as it does not harm another. To be true to the self means recognizing who you really are and then being true to that person. If your nature is one that yearns for simplicity and closeness with nature, you would not do well, for instance, as a stockbroker in New York.

Making a living and supporting a family is an honorable endeavor. What is not honorable is to lose the self while doing it. There is an "attitude" when we go about our daily business that does not lose sight of who we are, does not hand our power over to another or allow ourselves to accept the disrespect others may show us. It is an attitude of serenity, of knowing that we are a unique and wonderful expression of something that we may not understand, but we know exists. And, in that attitude of serenity, also exists the recognition that other beings are also unique and wonderful expressions of that "something" we don't understand. They may not be doing what we want them to do, but we still recognize the "essence" of who they are. According to **Webster's New Collegiate Dictionary, essence is: That in being which underlies all outward manifestations and is permanent and unchangeable.**

WE HAVE COME TO LEARN

That brings us to the theme that has been repeatedly present throughout this book—**the knowledge that we have come into the physical to experience life in its diversity; to learn from the experiences; to acquire even more knowledge, understanding and, hopefully, wisdom. Wisdom may be a state of being which refers to that "attitude of serenity" that does not lose sight of who we are even when we are in seemingly powerless and hopeless situations.** One of the lessons from many of the lifetimes reviewed in this book was to regain that sense of the self even when in seemingly impossible situations. **The lesson is to never lose sight of "who you are"—your essence.**

The theory is that we each have experienced many lifetimes as different races; different religions; as rich and poor; as murderer and saint; mother and prostitute. And, for what reason? Is it just to suffer? Or, is it to finally recognize the diversity of human experience; the range of emotions; the styles of living; **the final, ultimate oneness that we all share?**

Today, it is a small planet. If a child starves in Ethiopia, we know it or could know it. It affects us all. We can no longer plead ignorance about the pain and suffering of others simply because we have no contact with those people. In a matter of hours, usually, or days at the most, we can be anywhere on this planet. **All of us are members of the community of planet earth. All of us are part of the system of planet earth.** If one of us pollutes the air in our environment, we affect the air of the total environment.

THE POWER OF THOUGHTS

In earlier chapters we talked about the **power of thoughts. They have energy, vibration.** If the person next to you is full of hatred and angry thoughts, you can "feel" it. On the other hand, if the person next to you is very serene and balanced and thinking peaceful thoughts, you "feel" that, also. So, one could say that the presence of hateful, angry thoughts pollutes the environment and, therefore, pollutes the entire planet.

Imagine walking into a neighborhood inhabited by people who focus their lives on hatred and anger or fear. **Anger seems to be a response to fear.** Do you not think you would feel uncomfortable? Do you not think whole communities focused on hatred and fear would create discomfort on the planet? What of a community that unconditionally loves each individual, that celebrates the diversity of its members? How would you feel in that community? Would the energy from such a place not contribute to a more peaceful, loving feeling throughout the environment of the planet?

Yes, we are all connected. Our thoughts and feelings affect those around us and the planet as a whole. **To clear away our own fears, anger and arrogance allows us to feel more connected to our "core being," our spiritual Self, our High Self. By doing that we help create a better world.**

Alive Again...Again...and Again

Self as the Instrument of Knowledge

"Know Thyself." That advice has been repeated for thousands of years. Yet, when a generation started to explore the self, they were called "selfish" and "self-centered." One perceives the world through the self. **The self is the instrument through which you observe and interpret the events of a lifetime.** If you do not truly know the self, how can you make sense of what you have experienced. To know the self means to recognize the strengths, the weaknesses, the times when "automatic programming" is occurring. To be aware that some responses do not fit the occasion allows you to take back your power and control of your responses by reducing the impact of old, outmoded, no longer useful programming.

Old Tapes

As I stated in earlier chapters, much of the "automatic programming" or "computer programs" in our minds are believed by some of us to be the result of past-life experiences. **The programs exist for a reason—to give us information from which we acquire understanding and wisdom.** Once we understand why the program exists and what lesson we are to learn from that program, we are free to discard it and move on with our lives.

You do not always need to access your own exact tape or program. If you are aware when you observe situations in another person's life, or movies, or books or other past-life accounts that are similar to yours, you can learn the lesson and acquire the understanding and wisdom. In other words, **the purpose is to learn the lesson the experience offers.** If you can do that by reading about, or observing a similar situation that someone else experiences, then you are ahead of the game. After all, how many people do you know who keep getting themselves into the same messes and choose not to learn the lessons from their own experiences?

WHAT LESSONS?

So, what are these lessons we have come to learn? "**Compassion**" seems to be a big one; to recognize another's pain whether or not it is like your own; to recognize that even those who commit the most heinous of crimes are experiencing pain. After compassion comes "**forgiveness**." Perhaps it is necessary to feel compassion before one is able to forgive. **Forgiveness includes being able to forgive your own perceived weaknesses and shortcomings as well as those of another. When you are able to forgive, you are moving toward the unconditional love, the loving one another or treating one another as you would like to be treated.**

At that point the concept of brotherhood/sisterhood of beings, the oneness, becomes possible.

Index

Alive Again...Again...and Again

ORDER FORM

Awakening Publications

Fax Orders: **(602) 241-6633**

☎ *Telephone orders:*

Call Toll Free: 1 (800) 35-BOOKS
International Orders: (602) 650-8442
Have VISA or MasterCard numbers ready.

✉ *Postal orders send to:*

Awakening Publications,
C/O Thunderbird Fulfillment,
5501 North 7th Ave. Suite #116
Phoenix, AZ 85013-4700

For information call (602) 241-6677
Ask about our meditation tape and audio book.

Please send *Alive Again...Again...and Again.*

Company name: _____

Name: _____

Address: _____

City: _____ State: _____ Zip: _____

Telephone: ( ) _____

Book price: $12.95 plus shipping of $3.00 in U.S.
Please add sales tax for books shipped to Arizona addresses.

Payment:

☐ Check:
☐ Credit Card: ☐ VISA ☐ Master Card
Card number _____
Name on card: _____ exp. date: ____

CALL TOLL FREE AND ORDER NOW !